Reinventing Learning for the Always-On Generation

Strategies and Apps That Work

Ian Jukes

Ryan L. Schaaf

Nicky Mohan

Solution Tree | Press

a division of

Solution Tree

555 North Morton Street
Bloomington, IN 47404
800.733.6786 (toll free) / 812.336.7700
FAX: 812.336.7790
email: info@solution-tree.com
solution-tree.com

Printed in the United States of America

19 18 17 16 15   1 2 3 4 5

Library of Congress Cataloging-in-Publication Data

Jukes, Ian.

  Reinventing learning for the always-on generation : strategies and apps that work / by Ian Jukes, Ryan L. Schaaf, and Nicky Mohan.

      pages cm

  Includes bibliographical references and index.

  ISBN 978-1-936763-81-8 (perfect bound) 1. Educational technology. 2. Education--Effect of technological innovations on. I. Schaaf, Ryan L. II. Mohan, Nicky. III. Title.

  LB1028.3.J88 2015

  371.33--dc23

                            2015016019

Solution Tree
Jeffrey C. Jones, CEO
Edmund M. Ackerman, President

Solution Tree Press
President: Douglas M. Rife
Associate Acquisitions Editor: Kari Gillesse
Editorial Director: Lesley Bolton
Managing Production Editor: Caroline Weiss
Senior Production Editor: Suzanne Kraszewski
Proofreader: Ashante Thomas
Cover and Text Designer: Rachel Smith

The authors would like to dedicate this book to the loving memory of Dr. John Castellani, associate professor at Johns Hopkins University. His friendship and commitment to his students and family will never be forgotten.

I want to dedicate this book to the memory of my father, Arthur Jukes, my mother, Margaret Jukes, and my brother, John Jukes. You are gone but never forgotten. To my sisters, Cathy and Ann, thank you for helping me understand the meaning of family. To my friends Bruce Macdonald, Ted McCain, Frank Kelly, Richard Peck, and Jason Ohler, thanks for a lifetime of friendship. And to Nicky, who has put up with me through thick and thicker . . . my deepest sympathy.

—Ian Jukes

To my wonderful wife, Red—thank you for the privilege of being your husband and the gracious gifts of two beautiful, vibrant, and healthy little boys, Connor Brian and Ben Stephen. To my wonderful parents, Stephen and Susan Schaaf, for providing me with unconditional guidance, support, and love. To my successful sisters, Kristy and Sara, I thank you both for your determination and moxie. Finally, a huge thanks to my other family members, friends, and the Notre Dame of Maryland University community.

—Ryan L. Schaaf

This book is dedicated to Mini—my best friend, my love, my rock of support, my biggest fan. Mini, you left us peaceful memories. Your love is still our guide, and though we cannot see you, you are always by our side. To our daughter, Shona, and her partner, Shane, and our son, Sherwen—you continue to bless our home with love and have given our lives so much meaning. You have been my best cheerleaders. A special feeling of gratitude to my loving parents, Suraj and Chand—thank you for your unconditional love.

To Ian, thank you for never giving up on our friendship. You are there for everything—no bargaining or explanations needed. To Ethnie, I am so glad we met. You always listened and knew what to say. You are my inspiration. You will never be forgotten. And finally, to my sister Reena, her family, and my sister-in-law Fatima for your consistent encouragement and support.

—Nicky Mohan

Acknowledgments

We would like to thank Doug Reeves, Douglas Rife, Jason Ohler, Ted McCain, Delia Jenkins, and the Solution Tree team for their support and encouragement in the development of this project.

Solution Tree Press would like to thank the following reviewers:

Kristin Galle
Therapeutic Classroom Teacher
CESA #3
Fennimore, Wisconsin

Robert Pronovost
STEM Coordinator
Ravenswood City School District
East Palo Alto, California

James Kapptie
Director of Instructional Technology
Park County School District 6
Cody, Wyoming

Mandie Rainwater
World History / Psychology Teacher
Cypress Lake High School
Fort Myers, Florida

Table of Contents

Introduction

Chapter 1

Chapter 2

Chapter 3

Chapter 4

Chapter 5

Chapter 6

Chapter 7
Everyone Is Connected to Everyone and Everything............73

Chapter 8
Fast Pattern Reading............83

Chapter 9
Just-in-Case Versus Just-in-Time Learning............95

Chapter 10
Instant Versus Deferred Gratification............109

Chapter 11
Transfluency............121

Chapter 12

Chapter 13

About the Authors

Ian Jukes is the founder and executive director of the InfoSavvy Group, an international educational leadership consulting firm. He has been a teacher, school principal, district and provincial coordinator, writer, international consultant, university instructor, and keynote speaker. He has worked with clients in more than eighty countries and made more than ten thousand presentations. Ian has written or cowritten fifteen books and nine educational series. His most recent books are *Teaching the Digital Generation: No More Cookie-Cutter High Schools* (with Frank Kelly and Ted McCain, 2009), *Living on the Future Edge: Windows on Tomorrow* (with Ted McCain and Lee Crockett, 2010), *Understanding the Digital Generation: Teaching and Learning in the New Digital Landscape* (with Ted McCain and Lee Crockett, 2010), *Literacy Is Not Enough: 21st Century Fluencies for the Digital Age* (with Lee Crockett and Andrew Churches, 2011), and *Learning Without Classrooms* (with Frank Kelly and Ted McCain, 2015).

First and foremost, Ian is a passionate education evangelist. From the beginning of his education career, his focus has been on the compelling need to restructure our educational institutions so that they become relevant to the current and future needs of the digital generations —and to prepare learners for their future and not just our past.

To learn more about Ian's work, visit www.infosavvy21.com and follow him on Twitter @ijukes.

Ryan L. Schaaf is an assistant professor of educational technology at Notre Dame of Maryland University, and a faculty associate for the Johns Hopkins University School of Education Graduate Program. He has more than fifteen years of experience in the field of education. Before higher education, Ryan was a public school teacher, instructional leader, curriculum designer, and technology integration specialist in Maryland. In 2007, he was nominated as Maryland Teacher of the Year.

Ryan has published several research articles related to the use of digital games as an effective instructional strategy in the classroom in *New Horizons for Learning* and the *Canadian Journal of Action Research*. His first book, *Making School a Game Worth Playing: Digital Games in the Classroom*, which he coauthored with Nicky Mohan, was published in 2014. He is currently working with Nicky on the sequel tentatively titled *Game On: Using Digital Games for 21st Century Teaching, Learning, and Assessment*. Ryan enjoys presenting sessions and keynotes about the potential for gaming in the classroom, the characteristics of 21st century learning, and emerging technologies and trends in education.

To learn more about Ryan's work, visit www.infosavvy21.com or follow him on Twitter @RyanLSchaaf.

Nicky Mohan has been a classroom teacher, school and university administrator, instructional designer, business sector manager and trainer, and international speaker. At the University of Waikato, New Zealand, she designed and delivered courses and workshops based on research of best practices in teaching and learning. Since the early 2000s, she has made hundreds of presentations in more than a dozen countries.

Born in South Africa, a New Zealander by nationality, a Canadian by domicile, and a world citizen by choice, Nicky worked as the director of curriculum for the 21st Century Fluency Group, where she led a team of international writers in the development of curriculum materials that integrated 21st century skills into just-in-time teaching and learning (JiTTL) experiences that were relevant to both teachers and students. Nicky is currently the managing partner of LearningFutures21, an international educational consulting firm. Together with Ryan Schaaf, she has just published her first book, *Making School a Game Worth Playing: Digital Games in the Classroom*. She is currently working with Ryan on the sequel tentatively titled *Game On: Using Digital Games for 21st Century Teaching, Learning, and Assessment.*

To learn more about Nicky and her work, visit www.infosavvy21.com and follow her on twitter @nickymohan.

To book Ian Jukes, Ryan L. Schaaf, or Nicky Mohan for professional development, contact pd@solution-tree.com.

Foreword

Ted McCain, Associate Director for
Canada for the Thornburg Center

While it is not widely acknowledged today, teaching young people in school is a very challenging task. Teachers face mounting pressures in their classrooms that were not felt to nearly the same extent by their predecessors. Around the world, there has been a move like never before toward increased accountability for both student and teacher performance. Students as young as five years old, not to mention their teachers, are dealing with a multitude of government-mandated standardized tests. Required teaching of a standards-based curriculum has put a straitjacket on many teachers who want to foster creativity and higher-level thinking.

Along with the usual marking and preparation that come with instruction, teachers are facing increased demands on their time. Many schools give parents a teacher's email address, which makes it much easier for parents to contact teachers and request regular progress reports. When combined with the need to continually learn new instructional strategies and how to use new digital technologies to keep instruction relevant and engaging for modern students, many teachers face a greatly expanded daily workload.

In addition to all these challenges, the increasing frequency of family breakdowns places even more demands on teacher time. Teachers must help students with the fallout from problems at home before they can ever hope to effectively teach them. Unless you have actually been in the classroom on a daily basis, you really can't appreciate the new realities that many teachers face.

That is a major reason why I find this book so satisfying. It is clear that Ian Jukes, Ryan Schaaf, and Nicky Mohan have spent a great deal of time working with kids in the classroom, which makes what they have to say absolutely ring true. This book talks *with* teachers, not *at* them. What the authors highlight reflects one of the major issues affecting educators around the globe today: the impact that digital bombardment is having on the minds of young people in today's classrooms. This is an issue educators simply can't ignore.

Ian, Ryan, and Nicky point out that while on the outside kids today don't appear that much different from previous generations, there has been a profound change on the inside to their neurological makeup. This has happened because young people today are exposed to a digital world that was unimaginable to their parents and teachers when they were young.

The interconnected online world provides children today with immediate access to a wealth of digital multimedia experiences. This exposure is fundamentally altering the way kids today think about, engage with, and explore digital environments. From birth on, the always-on generation are completely immersed in, and take for granted, an informational world that most adults have never experienced. As a result, their minds have been profoundly and permanently affected by graphical communication via full-color images; the fast pace of online digital games; the increasing presentation of information in full motion and sound; the interconnected web of hyperlinked information sources; the instantaneous global reach of searches in the online world using tools like Google, YouTube, Facebook, Snapchat, and Twitter; and the ability to choose the direction and the pace of informational exploration. Their brains are literally bombarded by these digital experiences. As a result, kids today have become so adept at operating in this new digital landscape that they can do several digital multimedia tasks simultaneously. These kids are different indeed!

Having to teach in the age of digital bombardment has created an enormous challenge for teachers, particularly those who did not grow up with online digital experiences. How do you teach the digital generations? This is where Ian, Ryan, and Nicky really show their extensive educational backgrounds. The book is full of practical ideas about how to engage kids who have been fundamentally altered by online digital experiences. It is a lifeline for teachers dealing with all the pressures of modern classrooms who must now also figure out how to reach new generations of learners. This book is a great resource! You will want to refer to it again and again for practical ideas about how to teach these kids. I know I will. Enjoy!

A Changing World

We live in a world that has profoundly and fundamentally changed—one that continues to change in incomprehensible, ever-accelerating ways. As a result of this age of profound change, we face a fundamentally different kind of student—one whose experiences, expectations, and assumptions about the world we live in have already begun to force us to rethink teaching, learning, and assessment of that learning.

A few years back, Ian, Ted McCain, and Lee Crockett (2010) wrote a book titled *Understanding the Digital Generation: Teaching and Learning in the New Digital Landscape*, based in part on one thousand interviews Ian undertook with young people between the ages of five and twenty-five years old. What that book, and many more books just like it, and a great deal of academic research and personal experiences are telling us is this: as parents, as citizens, and particularly as educators, what we need to understand is that while, on the outside, kids today pretty much look the same as we did when we were growing up, on the inside, neurologically, today's digital generations are completely different from previous generations.

This is not just because today's children physically mature years earlier than kids did even fifteen years ago. It's not because of the clothes they choose to wear or because they might want to dye their hair and style it differently than we did. It's not because of the music they listen to or the way they talk. It's not because of what they say or how they act. What we now understand is that because of *digital bombardment*—pervasive exposure to digital technology, which primarily happens outside of school hours—kids' brains are literally being wired and rewired on an ongoing basis. In particular, digital bombardment is enhancing their visual memory, visual processing, and visual learning skills.

As Ian notes in *Understanding the Digital Generation* (Jukes, McCain, & Crockett, 2010), what researchers are now beginning to conclude is that our students are neurologically processing information in a fundamentally different way than the older generations do. This leaves many teachers wondering how to teach the kids of the digital generations. This book provides a pragmatic look at helping teachers do this one step at a time.

Reading This Book

You can read this book using two approaches: The traditional way is to start at the beginning and read until the end. If that strategy works for you, great! An alternative approach aligns with the way that many members of the digital generations prefer to learn; your entry point can be anywhere you want it to be. You can skim, scan, and scour the table of contents, or search the book itself for a topic you find interesting, relevant, or needed. Once you identify your starting point, you can dive right in. For example, if you are a classroom teacher facing the challenges of distracted and disengaged students, you might want to jump directly to chapter 4, "A Need for Speed," and continue examining the chapters pertaining to the attributes of digital learners and the strategies and tools that work in the classroom. If you are a parent, we recommend you start with chapter 2, "What's Wrong With Kids Today?" because it identifies and explains some of the common behaviors of today's digital generations. If you are a school administrator or educational leader, the logical place to start is chapter 1, "Curriculum Standards, the Common Core, and Beyond," because it addresses the eight-hundred-pound gorilla educators are facing today.

Regardless of your approach, you will find each chapter to be self-contained, starting with the identification of a core learning attribute for the digital generations. This is followed by a detailed explanation of the implications of this attribute to digital learners' learning preferences and styles. Then we provide a summary of specific strategies and tools that work for the learning attribute. Finally, we pose a series of discussion questions to consider as well as providing some recommendations for further reading and reference.

Let's get started.

Chapter 1

Curriculum Standards, the Common Core, and Beyond

Knowing content doesn't make you competent—
nor does understanding content. Competence is the
ability to apply content in some useful way.

—Anonymous

Peter Drucker (2008), management consultant, educator, and author, once wrote, "What gets measured gets done" (p. 321). Conversely, what doesn't get measured doesn't get done. Clearly, there is an increased focus on standards and accountability measures in education today. Many nations have put into place comprehensive academic performance standards to be attained by all students. Initiatives such as the United States' Common Core State Standards (CCSS), Australia's Australian Curriculum Assessment and Reporting Authority (ACARA), and New Zealand's National Standards identify a series of high-quality, academic standards for mathematics and English language arts, as well as other subject areas. The standards were created in an attempt to ensure that all students graduate from high school with the skills and knowledge necessary to be college or career ready.

Debate about standards has had an enormously polarizing effect on both political and educational conversations around the world. We need to acknowledge up front that it is unrealistic to disregard or dismiss the CCSS, or any other local, state, provincial, or national curricula. Standards are the destination; however, the road to achieving the standards has not been built for educators brick by brick. While the standards dictate *what* must be taught, they do not prescribe *how* it must be taught. If we know where we want to go, there are many different roads we can follow to reach our destination. There will always be a need to learn content, but there are multiple ways to introduce it. For content to stick, educators must be able to make connections to the real world, while at the same time making the content interesting and relevant to students.

Richard Saul Wurman (1989), the cofounder of the highly regarded TED conferences, once commented that "learning can be seen as the acquisition of knowledge. But before learning can take place, it must be of interest—that interest precedes learning. In order to acquire and remember new knowledge, it must stimulate curiosity in some way" (p. 87). Wurman said that learning is like Velcro. Only one side of learning is made up of facts; the other consists of stories, ideas, experiences, and personal interest. Wurman says presenting content to students without personal interest or relevance is like having only one side of a piece of Velcro—the content just doesn't stick.

When adopting standards such as the Common Core, and while keeping in mind the needs of 21st century learners, teachers can exercise their creativity to deliver instruction in dynamic and engaging ways. As our good friend Douglas Reeves states,

> The most powerful educational strategies and approaches are not those that merely keep up with the latest version of standards, but those that transcend every version of standards. If we had no standards and no national, provincial, or state mandates, the question would be, What is the right thing to do for students in the 21st century? We want our students to pursue digital fluency, critical thinking, and creativity, not because it is required by law, but because it is absolutely essential for the future world in which our students will live. (personal communication, April 10, 2014)

If educators are to be successful and make learning relevant to the lives of the digital generations, then they can no longer only be content dispensers. The secret to success in any classroom has very little to do with being a good content dispenser or classroom manager, and everything to do with creating an engaging methodology that compels students to want to be there. It's not about *making* students learn; it's about *getting them to want* to learn. Without motivation, there will be no learning.

Students are increasingly disengaged and continue to leave both high schools and universities in disturbingly high numbers. According to the High School Survey of Student Engagement (HSSSE) conducted by the Indiana University Center for Evaluation and Education Policy (CEEP) (Indiana University School of Education, 2010), 42 percent of respondents said they thought of dropping out (of schools) because they didn't see the value in the work they were asked to do. This is happening in part because students see the disconnect between our focus on content recall rather than demonstrating competency through the application of content to solve real-world problems. The reality is that the goals of schools are increasingly misaligned with the demands of the global marketplace.

If we are to stay relevant and fulfill our dual mandate of preparing students to be successful on exams and for their future beyond school, our focus must shift to providing them with what they need. We passionately believe that education cannot just be about the standards that are the driving force and primary fixation of schools today.

The New Basics

So what are the critical skills all students need to be successful both in school and in life beyond school? We have interviewed hundreds of parents, as well as business, political, community, and educational leaders from around the world. They have consistently identified a comprehensive list of essential skills. We have come to call this list the *new basics*. The new basics are the skills above and beyond being able to do well on a written exam that all students must cultivate to prepare themselves for success in the world that awaits them once they leave school. (See figure 1.1.)

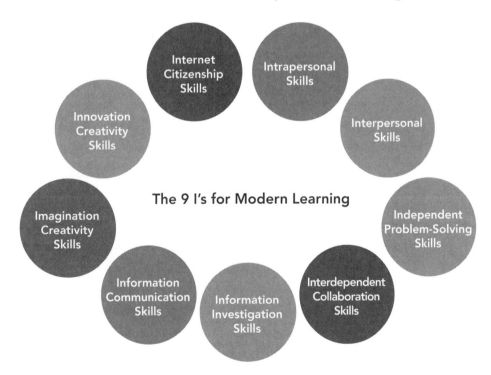

Source: McCain, 2015. Used with permission.

Figure 1.1: The new basics for success in the future.

The new basics are made up of what our friend and colleague Ted McCain (2015) calls the "9 I's": intrapersonal skills, interpersonal skills, independent problem-solving skills, interdependent collaboration skills, information investigation skills, information communication skills, imagination creativity skills, innovation creativity skills, and Internet citizenship skills.

We Can Have It All

The CCSS will continue to be assessed using high-stakes testing. However, having standards and standardized testing doesn't mean that we have to teach in a standardized way. A test score is only a one-dimensional indicator of learning. If all we do is teach to the tests, all we're going to get is a test score. We must teach past the test by consistently infusing the new basics into our teaching and learning strategies. That way, we will get the desired test results, while simultaneously cultivating the new basics in our students and being able to authentically assess student learning. That's what Velcro learning is all about.

Authentic assessment might include students writing, describing, explaining, designing, planning, organizing, leading, persuading, negotiating, teaching, modeling, implementing, demonstrating, performing, building, or producing authentic products. Authentic assessment requires learners independently or collaboratively to execute one or more of these complex processes, as well as to generate evidence that they have done so.

The real goal of assessment must be to improve deep and meaningful student learning. This goal can be accomplished through using portfolios, oral and multimedia presentations, and reviews by experts and peers. All of these can be used to improve documentation and understanding of learning, and to provide more detailed feedback for both teachers and students. Such methods provide a more complete and continuous picture of student learning, helping teachers and students monitor progress and model different ways adults improve performance in life.

Strategies and Tools That Work

So, in fact, we can have it all. We can simultaneously address both short-term learning goals and long-term life and career goals. We can have success on today's mandated exams, while also helping our students develop the skills they need for tomorrow. We can do this by:

Tapping into student interest and relevance

Making real-world connections

Showing students how to ask good questions

Showing students how to reflect on their learning (debriefing)

Encouraging risk taking

Promoting collaborative practices for both teachers and students

Tapping Into Student Interest and Relevance

Students learn more effectively when they already know something about a content area and when concepts in that area have meaning to them and their background or culture. When teachers link new information to a student's prior knowledge, they activate interest and curiosity and infuse instruction with a sense of purpose. Students learn and remember new information best when it is linked to relevant prior knowledge. Furthermore, teachers who link classroom activities and instruction to prior knowledge build on their students' familiarity with a topic and enable students to *connect the curriculum content* to their own culture and experience (Beyer, 1991).

We expect students to be active learners through engagement. They acquire new knowledge, apply what they have learned, and continuously build on their existing knowledge base. Interest-driven learning, with a focus on projects that are relevant to individual students, is the key. To do this, we must move the learning experience from students *doing* projects to students learning *through* projects.

Students find that it is easier to learn content when it is relevant to their lives. Relevance is important to teaching and learning because it is directly related to student engagement and motivation (Frymier & Schulman, 1995; Martin & Dowson, 2009). We often find that the curriculum contains topics that students consider boring. Our task as educators is to add relevance to otherwise uninteresting content by adding in elements that grab the students' attention.

How do you cultivate personal interest and relevance? The following example shows what it looks like. Getting students interested in geography, history, environmental science, or political issues can be a great challenge. Students often just don't see the relevance, which makes it hard to pique their interest. It's a challenge to get them engaged. But when you talk about these topics within the context of a movie like *Avatar*, it immediately grabs students' attention.

Let's take a moment to consider all the themes or issues that *Avatar* can address: culture clash, civilizations, colonialism, capitalism, war, geography, unrequited love, geology, astronomy, belief systems, technology, cloning, racism, environmentalism, eco-terrorism, science fiction, science fact, journeys of self-discovery—the list of possible themes is endless, an absolute treasure trove of interesting and relevant topics: popular games, movies, cartoons, books, songs, sports, world events, websites, community issues.

By creating an engaging methodology through relevance and interest, students' curiosity is aroused—they want to know more. Without engagement, there will be no learning—at least not the learning we want. Without engagement, students discover two indelible lessons: "School is boring," and "I'm a failure here." It's about encouraging students to take their learning beyond the confines of the classroom—to fulfill their personal interests and curiosity while at the same time meeting the set curriculum objectives. If you can interest them, excite them, engage them, and challenge them—if you can make topics relevant to their lives—then test scores will inevitably improve. So interest and relevance are an essential element of addressing standards.

Making Real-World Connections

Learning is not just confined to a classroom. In fact, learning can occur at home, on a bus, at a coffee shop, in the supermarket—just about anywhere. John Dewey once wrote, "The school must represent present life—life as real and vital to the child as that which he carries on in the home, in the neighborhood, or on the playground" (as quoted in Powers, 2010).

If our job as educators is to prepare students for the real world, why not start by having students solve real-world problems or perform real-world tasks? By making real-world connections to otherwise uninteresting or abstract concepts dictated by the curriculum, students can make meaning of content they are introduced to. If we want students to operate at the highest level of Bloom's taxonomy, we must ensure that they are able to see the relationship between concepts taught in class and current, real-world contexts.

Making real-world connections is best suited for project-based learning environments, where students work and communicate collaboratively to find solutions to problems or complete relevant tasks. Instead of depending primarily on traditional tests, exams, and quizzes, student projects and tasks become critical evidence of their learning at each step of the process.

Projects framed in a scenario are a powerful way to arouse curiosity and motivate or pique student interest. Within a scenario, students are presented with a real-world problem or challenge in the form of an essential question that requires the application of higher-order thinking skills. To solve the problem, students are required to complete multiple tasks and activities that are correlated to skills and knowledge identified in the curriculum. We can teach virtually any topic within a subject by using a scenario from the real world.

For example, using a recent human-made or natural disaster as a scenario, we could set our students up with a challenge: *Armed with your newly found knowledge about a particular human-made or natural disaster, what can you do to help rebuild the devastated community?* This kind of project can cover more than just one subject area. While this may initially look more like a scenario used to teach geography, teachers can also use it in language arts for teaching speaking, listening, reading, and writing.

Scenarios like this provide students with the opportunity to hold meaningful discussions and learn new content within the confines of the classroom, while at the same time being actively involved in world events in positive, constructive ways. Students learn geography, science, and perhaps mathematics, while cultivating an awareness of what it means to be a global digital citizen.

But such projects touch on much more than just the lives of students. They also help people in need elsewhere around the world. Even when using this model only part of the time, students learn both content and context. It addresses both the information needed to be successful on exams and the processes that students will use repeatedly in their lives.

Showing Students How to Ask Good Questions

Albert Einstein said, "The important thing is not to stop questioning. Curiosity has its own reason for existing." One of the keys to Einstein's genius was his determination to "never lose a holy curiosity"—to never stop questioning. As teachers, we ask most of the questions written or orally, and our students are expected to provide the answers. Questions are primarily used to assess student understanding or, in the case of oral questioning, for organizational purposes—to check students' classwork and homework, review and summarize lessons, and evaluate students' learning (Black, 2001; Goodman & Berntson, 2000; Wilen, 1985).

If we want to fulfill our obligation for teaching the new basics, we must begin by showing our students how to ask good questions. Students will ask questions about things they are interested in or curious about. Being able to ask good questions helps with student engagement and interest, develops students' thinking skills, stimulates students to inquire and investigate independently, helps them synthesize information and experiences, creates a context for exploring new ideas, and enhances students' cumulative knowledge base (Black, 2001; Goodman & Berntson, 2000; Hyman & Schuh, 1974).

For students to succeed in project-based learning, they must be able to formulate their own powerful questions based on existing knowledge, motivation, and curiosity. We can move students from asking lower-order questions that simply require yes or no answers (or can be answered using Google) to asking powerful questions that require higher-order thinking.

For example, asking "Is a survival kit essential?" generates a yes or no answer. "What is in a survival kit?" can be googled. Using a search engine to find the contents of a survival kit is a good starting point, but "What can I do to help my family prepare a survival kit for a disaster?" requires higher-order thinking skills. The knowledge gained from the research must now be analyzed and then applied to solve the real-world challenge of coming up with creative ways to help a family prepare a survival kit for a disaster.

How do you get students to generate powerful questions? Use a "wonder wall" where students are encouraged to use sticky notes to post questions about their learning on one side of the wall and questions about things they are interested in or curious about on the other. A wonder wall helps foster independence and makes the students think a little more about their questions. At a glance, the teacher is able to make a quick visual judgment about what questions he or she has time to address or may want to prioritize. It is also helpful in giving constructive formative feedback to students. To paraphrase the great educational philosopher Neil Postman, children enter school as a question mark and exit as a period (Postman & Weingartner, 1969). (Personally, we think our job is to help students leave as exclamation marks.)

Showing Students How to Reflect on Their Learning (Debriefing)

Reflection, sometimes also referred to as *debriefing*, is the bridge between experiences and learning. We usually refer to this as *metacognition*—"thinking about thinking." Reflection is an essential new basic for students. Once they are able to think about their thinking, they can "learn how to learn."

In the real world outside of school, responsibility for work continues long after the development of an initial product. It's a cyclical process of refining the initial design. But in education, instructors traditionally do most of the evaluation. As a result, students quickly get the idea that work is a linear process that begins with an assignment and ends when they hand something in.

If we are going to adequately prepare students for the world ahead, we need to move beyond just quantitative, summative assessment of learning. We have to move to qualitative, formative assessment, to peer assessment, to self-assessment, and to community assessment. It's critical that we get our students involved at every stage of the evaluation of their work because group assessment, peer assessment, and self-assessment foster personal ownership and accountability of the learning.

Debriefing/reflection/metacognitive skills include revisiting each stage of the process and reflecting critically on both the process undertaken and the product created: identifying what was learned, how it was learned, and how we can make the product or process better the next time around, and then acting on those reflections, internalizing the new learning, and transferring that learning to both familiar and different circumstances in the future.

Debriefing or reflection can take place before, during, and after a project. Students can learn to reflect through the use of questions. To prompt student reflection, teachers can ask guiding questions that help students during the debrief stage and give students specific feedback about their reflections. Debriefing is an essential skill in both school and life and must be used as a critical teaching and learning strategy.

Encouraging Risk Taking

Syndicated columnist Doug Larson wrote, "To err is human; to admit it, superhuman" (Kumar, 2005, p. 231). Indeed, we live and learn in a society where mistakes are often met with ridicule and scorn.

> All of us make mistakes. If we're fortunate, we catch them ourselves (or someone else does), and we do our best to correct them. Typically, we make mistakes through lack of attention. But once they're pointed out to us, we immediately recognize them and usually know the corrective action to take. Our students do this as well. (Fisher & Frey, 2010, p. 1)

Gamers spend 80 percent of their time failing, yet still have positive experiences and retain positive emotions despite those failures. Why? "When you're able to fail 80 percent of the time, and you're able to draw on those positive emotions, you're able to get to the positive place you want" (Ryssdal, 2011). Allowing students to fail in school, and leveraging games' motivating factors, can boost student engagement and also teach students one of today's most sought-after skills: problem solving. Teachers and parents must help the digital generations understand that failure is a part of the learning process—one that is quite powerful. The gaming model challenges traditional assumptions about how success is measured in schools. In the traditional model, failing 80 percent of the time would lead to a failing letter grade, not to mention discouraged learners. With the gaming model, success is measured on a formative, cumulative basis. There is less emphasis placed on mistakes made on the way and more on the end result.

Failure forces the person to think critically of his or her mistakes and avoid making them in the future by reflecting on solutions. If failure was considered the end of the line, Thomas Edison would never have invented the lightbulb, J. K. Rowling would never have published the adventures of Harry Potter at Hogwarts School of Witchcraft and Wizardry, and no one would have heard of Michael Jordan, a high school student cut from his basketball team. In essence, failure forges great people—the type of people we need in an age of disruptive change and fundamental uncertainty.

The perfect incubator for students living in an age of fundamental uncertainty is problem-based learning. As educators and parents, it is difficult to watch our charges fail. It is built into our DNA to help the young. The classroom (and the home for that matter) must be a space where failure is a learning experience. By crafting learning experiences into challenges where the potential pathway to fail exists, we, as educators, have the chance to help our students get beyond anger, frustration, and embarrassment to develop better 21st century survival skills such as perseverance, adaptability, self-reflection, and tenacity.

If teachers wish to develop their students' risk-taking abilities, they must provide them with learning experiences with unknown solutions, forcing students to risk being right or wrong. Teachers can provide these opportunities through scenario-based learning, project-based learning, or problem-based learning. These forms of learning are messy and unpredictable; teachers and students are unsure of what the experiences will hold for them. Students are required to perform their own research, locate their own resources to formulate their solutions to these challenges, and prepare a product to demonstrate their mastery of the content while working alone or in collaborative teams.

Do these steps seem familiar? That is because if you visit any Fortune 500 company, you will see the successful, driven employees performing the same steps in their jobs. These learning experiences, filled with uncertainty, will foster risk taking for students in a real-world context.

The CCSS demand critical and creative thinking. These essential 21st century skills are needed to solve these challenges with unknown solutions. By fostering the new basics, educators will prepare students for the uncertainties of the ever-changing, unpredictable global market.

Promoting Collaborative Practices for Both Teachers and Students

Teachers can't operate in silos of isolation. Successful lessons and teaching strategies must be shared in the school building as well as global professional learning communities. Teachers have flocked to Twitter and Pinterest to explore and share success stories. Despite factors such as high-stakes testing, lack of financial resources, and foreign competition, the teaching profession remains one of the best industries for sharing trade secrets because the payoff equals a prosperous future for students. Teachers must actively seek out professional learning communities to learn from, share with, and network in. Use groups of like-minded educators to work through ideas and to find inspiration.

In the past, seeking out these communities might have involved going to a conference once a year or a district meeting every semester. Teachers have an extreme shortage of time. They can't research the best practices or locate the perfect resource for each class easily. Having local, regional, and global professional learning communities brings together educators to share success stories, lesson suggestions, resources, and news.

Students also learn by applying their newfound knowledge to similar and different situations. As wonderful as today's classrooms are, powerful learning can occur outside of the traditional classroom setting. The surrounding communities are calling for students to volunteer for worthwhile service projects. Community advocacy, environmental projects, and philanthropic programs help students apply their citizenship practices to benefit the community.

Students and teachers can also tie their experiential and service learning initiatives into content-area curriculums by looking for learning opportunities in the moment. For instance, if a famous landmark like an old building is being torn down in the local community, in some instances the school community will rally to preserve it. In this situation, teachers can incorporate local history, persuasive writing, community outreach, volunteerism, and civics.

Summarizing the Main Points

This section provides readers with a recap of important information covered in the chapter.

- It is unrealistic to ignore the CCSS, or any other local, state, provincial, or national curricula.

- For content to stick, educators must be able to make connections to the real world, while at the same time making the content interesting and relevant to students.

- The most powerful educational strategies and approaches are not those that merely keep up with the latest version of standards, but those that transcend every version of standards.

- The new basics are the skills above and beyond being able to do well on a written exam that all students must cultivate in order to prepare themselves for the world that awaits them once they leave school.

- The real goal of assessment must be to improve deep and meaningful student learning as reflected by portfolios, oral and multimedia presentations, and reviews by experts and peers.

Questions to Consider

Now that you've finished the chapter, consider the following questions.

1. What would happen if students were allowed to follow their curiosities, with time allotted and teacher support provided during the regular school day?

2. Is school a place or a process? Explain your answer.

3. Who changes first—the teacher or the student? Explain your thinking.

4. What will students need to know and be able to do to function now and in the future?

5. What teaching and learning strategies can you incorporate into your daily practices to provide interesting and relevant experiences for your students?

Reference and Resource Roundup

In a traditional book, the references and resources are provided at the end of each chapter or at the end of the book. Increasingly, in the digital age, references and resources include both paper and web-based content. Have you ever clicked on a web link and found that what you are looking for has moved or no longer exists? What's available today might vanish tomorrow. So, after a long discussion and some experimentation, we decided to try something very different with this book.

We used a free, online tool called Evernote to curate all of the online references, resources, and documents that we had gathered while researching and writing the book. We then catalogued these materials on a chapter-by-chapter basis in a public access Evernote notebook we created. This collection will be regularly reviewed and updated with new and relevant content. To view these documents, just click on the following link and select the "View Notebook" option.

http://bit.ly/Attributes_of_Digital_Learners

If you have a suggestion for an article that you think should be added to this collection, contact us at InfoSavvy21 at www.infosavvy21.com.

Chapter 2

What's Wrong With Kids Today?

For the digital generations, the past is a foreign country.

—LARRY ZIMMERMAN (ADAPTED BY IAN JUKES)

Back in the 1960s in the popular stage musical *Bye Bye Birdie*, the lyrics to the song "Kids" included "Kids! I don't know what's wrong with these kids today. Kids! Who can understand anything they say? Kids! . . . Why can't they be like we were, perfect in every way? . . . They are just impossible to control!" (It's ironic to note that the same people who were being criticized over fifty years ago in that song are now criticizing the younger generations.)

You hear it everywhere:

- "What's wrong with kids today?"
- "Kids just aren't as smart as they were when I was young."
- "Students today can't read and write the way students did twenty years ago."
- "Kids today don't have any social skills."
- "All these kids want to do is play with their cell phones and video games."
- "When I ask students for the capital city of Peru, they say they don't know— they want to google it. What's Google got to do with learning anyway?"
- "Kids today just can't concentrate the way that we used to."
- "Children can't or won't sit and listen."

These are just a few of the many responses we've heard when talking to adults about the digital generations. Many teachers express great concern about their students' lack of ability to learn the way students did in the past. We especially hear this from teachers who have been teaching for a long period of time. Many complain their traditional teaching methods are just not as effective with students in classrooms today as they once were.

One of the most frequent comments we get from adults is that there appears to be a complete lack of balance between the digital and nondigital lives of young people today. Many of them appear to spend significant periods of their time outside of school texting; connecting with Snapchat, Instagram, and other social networks; and surfing the Internet while simultaneously playing games on an Xbox, iPad, or smartphone.

Concerns have been expressed about the increasing amounts of time the digital generations engage with their tools. There are those who even suggest that these tools are dumbing down our students and diminishing their ability to think for themselves. While we acknowledge that there are concerns, adults must realize that the children of the digital age use these tools in a manner that goes well beyond the ways we used traditional tools like paper, pencils, or a chalkboard. The challenge we face is understanding how these tools can be leveraged in a manner that interests and engages digital learners.

This book identifies the strengths and weaknesses of various digital tools and discusses how they can be effectively used for teaching, learning, and assessment. But beyond this, the real value of this book is that it is intended to help the reader better understand and engage with today's digital generations.

The Technological Alteration of the Modern Mind

A major theme of this book is that the digital world is fundamentally changing the way children think. Their brains are constantly being altered by the audiovisual and interactive experiences provided by new, online digital tools.

A number of books have been written about the impact of technology on digital culture. One of the most provocative is *iBrain: Surviving the Technological Alteration of the Modern Mind* by neuroscientists Gary Small and Gigi Vorgan (2008). It examines the remarkable development of the human brain caused by the impact of today's emerging technologies. *iBrain* contrasts the neural processing skills of the digital generations with those of the older generations and proposes that the new digital landscape is dramatically rewiring young minds. Another related book is *Brain Rules:*

12 Principles for Surviving and Thriving at Work, Home, and School by John Medina (2008). Medina's book puts a strong emphasis on the impact of digital technology on young minds. Both of these books address some of the major concerns related to the excessive use of digital tools.

Small and Vorgan (2008) begin their book with the following statement:

> Daily exposure to high technology—computers, smartphones, video games, search engines like Google and Yahoo—stimulates brain cell alteration and neurotransmitter release, gradually strengthening new neural pathways in our brains while weakening old ones. Because of the current technological revolution, our brains are evolving right now—at a speed like never before. (p. 1)

This rapid alteration of the brain has been so dramatic that traditional thinking about cognitive development is proving inadequate to describe what is occurring in the brains of children today. Nineteenth-century Swiss psychologist Jean Piaget made observations well over one hundred years ago about children's cognitive development. His comments have been useful in understanding what is going on inside children's brains as they age. However, the rapid evolution of the brain that is occurring today, particularly in light of the emergence of the new digital landscape, is causing researchers to re-examine some of Piaget's observations about early cognitive development.

Small and Vorgan (2008) make the following statement regarding the dramatic changes in the brains of children today:

> Piaget charted these milestones to adulthood, beginning with the first two years of life, when a toddler develops awareness of other people and learns to relate to them. From two to six years, the young child learns basic language skills. However, the thinking is relatively concrete until the teen years, when the ability for abstract thought and reason takes hold. If digital technology continues to distract young susceptible minds at the present rate, the traditional developmental stages will need to be redefined. (p. 28)

Such a redefinition will need to more accurately describe what is happening in the brains of young children as their minds respond to the new experiences provided by digital tools. This redefinition must also highlight the growing concerns being expressed as to whether important cognitive milestones are being delayed—or even missed entirely—as children grow up in a digital culture. Many of the advanced skills children develop while using digital tools empower them to do things that were unimaginable just a few short years ago. At the same time, there is growing concern that other essential cognitive skills are not being developed, because it appears that many in the digital generations devote too much attention to their digital worlds to the exclusion of traditional, nondigital activities.

In particular, many experts assert that one essential skill area that is being under-developed in the digital culture is face-to-face interpersonal interaction. The digital generations appear to be spending an increasing amount of time cultivating online virtual relationships using digital tools and less time interacting with real people in face-to-face relationships. A major concern being expressed is what this decreased interpersonal interaction is doing to brain development and the acquisition of face-to-face interpersonal skills. As Small and Vorgan (2008) point out, "without enough face-to-face interpersonal stimulation, a child's neural circuits can atrophy, and the brain may not develop normal interactive social skills" (p. 27). They continue:

> Recent neuroscience points to pathways in the brain that are neces-sary to hone interpersonal skills, empathetic abilities, and effective personal instincts. In the digital generation, which has been raised on technology, these interpersonal neural pathways are often left unstimulated and underdeveloped. (Small & Vorgan, 2008, p. 117)

It is clear that skills in creating and maintaining virtual relationships are essential in the modern world. At the same time, it is also clear that these skills must be bal-anced with doing the same things in face-to-face relationships if young people are going to have satisfying and productive interactions with others, both personally and professionally.

The increasing amount of time that kids spend using their digital tools is having negative effects on several areas of their development. There is great concern that young people are not getting enough physical exercise. Coupled with the lack of physical activity, there is legitimate concern that they are not gaining an appreciation for nature and being in the outdoors. Many parents and teachers worry that young people are not spending enough time reading for pleasure, or reading at all for that matter. There are concerns that the highly addictive nature of computer games and online adventure sites and the interactive nature of most digital activities are creating such obsessive behavior in kids that it meets the definition of a clinical addiction.

These are just a few of the many concerns that have been raised over the effects of the digital world on the minds and behavior of people deeply immersed in digital culture. New digital tools provide powerful ways for getting things done, and devel-oping skills in using them is essential in the modern world. But while acquiring these skills is important, young people must have balance in their lives to develop into fully functional and productive friends, spouses, partners, colleagues, and citizens.

The Need for Balance in the Lives of Children and Adults Alike

We must remember that balance goes both ways. Adults—parents, teachers, administrators, school district staff, community members, and politicians—are all involved in making decisions about what students will learn, how they will learn, where they will learn, what programs will be offered, what equipment will be used, and how student performance will be evaluated. In the same way that we have every right to expect the digital generations to respect, understand, and engage with our world and our values, we must also take the time and effort to respect, understand, and engage with their world and their values. Just because the older generations were here first doesn't mean they and we can ignore the world of the digital generations. It doesn't mean that our ways are better. And, believe us, we ignore their world at our peril. What we desperately need is balance—balance between our world and theirs and between traditional and digital learning environments.

How can we expect 21st century students to remain engaged in schools based on 20th century tools and traditional ideas about what learning looks like? In reality, as our friend Doug Reeves (personal communication, June 30, 2014) points out to us, "Actually, it's more like 15th and 19th century learning. For that matter, the Lyceum of 350 BCE was more engaging and interactive than many 21st century classrooms." How can we expect students to see the relevance of instructional approaches that target outdated skills taught in an outdated manner? How can we hope to connect with the digital generations when the examples we use in our learning materials and our instruction come from a nondigital time they have never experienced and thus can't relate to? How can we think we are adequately preparing students for life in the 21st century if we ourselves have not learned how the 21st century world really operates? And how can we expect our students to follow our advice about how they should conduct themselves in the modern world when we ourselves have not engaged with their world in any meaningful way?

This is not about preparing students for the 21st century. This is about preparing today's students for the new realities of an ever-changing world, and the new basics we will all need to effectively function in the new digital landscape.

There is an urgent need for balance in the lives of young people today. The digital generations must learn to engage effectively with both online and offline worlds. But in the same way that the digital generations need to find balance between their world and ours, there is also a desperate need for balance in the lives of those adults who are presently making critical decisions that will affect the lives and futures of the digital generations.

What is needed is a balance that acknowledges the realities of the digital online world—that kids are way ahead of us in understanding the new digital landscape and that we have a lot to learn before we can apply our life experiences to safely and effectively guide our students through this new digital world. That's exactly what our goal is in writing this book.

The Challenge of Change: The "Educentric" View

We end this chapter by acknowledging that we face a great challenge in writing this book. That's because when we consider the target reading audience, what we understand intuitively—what we know unconsciously—is that the vast majority of the people reading this book have spent almost their entire lives in the classroom.

As students, teacher interns, teachers, and perhaps administrators, we've all spent a minimum of seventeen years inside the traditional classroom—inside what we call the "educentric" box. This applies to even our youngest teachers. Because of our experiences inside the educentric box, many of us have had very little opportunity, very little need, to understand what's going on outside of education—where there are things happening that hold enormous implications for students and for those of us who work inside education. And because we've spent such a large portion of our lives inside the educentric box, it's absolutely certain we all suffer from a terrible affliction. It's called terminal paradigm paralysis.

What's a paradigm? A *paradigm* is a mindset, a perspective, a worldview, a way of looking for meaning in the world. Most people only see as far as their own experiences. A paradigm is incredibly powerful because it can prevent us from seeing things from other points of view. Our paradigm is often the reason for doing something we can no longer think of a reason for doing. Our paradigms are an everyday, unconscious, taken-for-granted part of our lives. And our educational paradigms can compel us to do things in the same way they have traditionally been done, despite the fact the world might have changed just a little bit in the meantime. There's nothing worse than getting caught with your paradigm down.

The real challenge in reading this book is to allow yourself to step outside your educentrism—to step beyond your existing paradigms about teaching, learning, and assessment, and consider how we can leverage our students' digital learning preferences to transform education.

Summarizing the Main Points

This section provides readers with a recap of important information from the chapter.

- There is a serious lack of balance in the lives of kids today.

- The rapid evolution of the brain that is occurring due to digital technology is causing many experts to reconsider the validity of traditional thought on cognitive development.

- One important skill area that is underdeveloped in a digital culture is face-to-face interpersonal interaction.

- Children today need to balance multitasking skills with strategies for developing single-tasking skills. They must cultivate their ability to focus and complete one task at a time.

- Adults today need to balance their nondigital life experiences with new digital experiences.

- Failure to acknowledge the new digital landscape may have catastrophic consequences for education.

Questions to Consider

Now that you've finished the chapter, consider the following questions.

1. How has your world changed in the past ten years? How is your life different now than it was then?

2. What technology do you use today that you didn't have ten years ago?

3. How many of those new technologies can you now carry with you?

4. What devices and services that once required a human operator have now been automated?

5. How has the appearance of this new digital landscape affected you, your family, your community, and your workplace?

6. What are some general concerns the older generations have about the digital generations?

7. How can the digital generations strike a balance between their digital and nondigital lives?

For up-to-date resource materials related to this chapter, please visit http://bit.ly/Attributes_of_Digital_Learners.

Chapter 3

Kids Are Different

We already knew that kids learned computer technology more easily than adults. It is as if children were waiting all these centuries for someone to invent their native language.

—Jaron Lanier

The numbers are staggering. Every minute of the day, YouTube users upload 100 hours of new video, email users send 204 million messages (Knoblauch, 2014), Google receives over 4 million search queries, Facebook users share 2,460,000 pieces of content, Tinder users swipe 416,667 times, WhatsApp users share 347,222 photos, Twitter users tweet 277,000 comments, Instagram users post 16,000 new photos, Amazon makes $83,000 in online sales, Pandora users listen to 61,141 hours of music, Apple users download 48,000 apps, Yelp users post 26,380 reviews, Skype users connect for 23,300 hours of video calls, Vine users share 8,333 videos, and Pinterest users pin 3,472 images. There are many excellent sources for statistics out there, but some really good ones include http://bits.blogs.nytimes.com, www.intel .com, www.apple.com, http://time.com, www.dailymail.co.uk, www.skype.com, and www.statisticbrain.com.

For some readers, it may sound as if we're speaking a foreign language. Regardless, we simply can't ignore what's happening in the new digital landscape, because it is having such a profound impact on all of our lives today.

Digital Bombardment

The book *Understanding the Digital Generation* (Jukes et al., 2010) makes the observation that while externally kids look the same as previous generations, they are neurologically different because of *digital bombardment*—the inescapable exposure to digital technologies. Digital bombardment has created the always-on generation:

generations of children, tweens, teens, and adults that text, game, surf the web, and use Instagram, Snapchat, Facebook, and Twitter to connect to everyone and everything. This is happening regardless of race, culture, socioeconomics, and geography. (See figure 2.1.)

Figure 2.1: Digital bombardment.

To explain chronic digital bombardment, let's start by attempting to quantify and qualify what we mean by digital bombardment. According to a Viacom Nickelodeon report, in the United States, between birth and age six, kids look at one or more screens for an hour and twenty minutes a day. And these measurements don't even address indirect exposure to screens, which puts the amount of time a screen is on in the foreground or background at nearly four hours a day for kids ages eight months to eight years (Nickelodeon, 2013).

Love it or hate it, screen culture is a foundational element of contemporary childhood. The digital generations live a three-screen lifestyle. This includes any combination of TV, computer, tablet, and cell phone. And they're using these different devices to build very complex and deep modes of communication with one another. This is the always-on generation.

According to the National Association of State Boards of Education (NASBE), in the United States, on average, kids today spend more than eighty hours a week using one, two, or more screens simultaneously—as opposed to about twenty-five hours a week they spend attending school. As a result, they spend more than three times the amount of time they spend at school using their digital devices. They have gone from being teenagers to screenagers. Of those eighty-plus hours a week, they spend an average of thirty-five hours online. Ten percent spend more than one hundred hours a week (Baker, n.d.).

And it's women, not men, who are the power users. Women in the United States use the Internet 17 percent more each month than their male counterparts. Women are more likely to own and be using their mobile phones. They spend more time talking on them and spend more time sending text messages. Women are the fastest-growing and largest users on Skype, and that's mostly younger women. Women are the fastest-growing category and most frequent users of every social networking site with the exception of LinkedIn (Madrigal, 2012). They are also sending more than 4,000 text messages per month (The Nielsen Company, 2010). That's more than 135 text messages a day, or 8 for every waking hour. Male numbers are only slightly less. And by the way, a few years back, a teen by the name of Brady James from Los Angeles sent 217,541 text messages in a single month (Hansen, 2011). To put these numbers into perspective, he sent an average of 4.8 text messages *every minute* of every hour of every day for an entire month.

Texting continues to grow in popularity because it promotes communication, cooperation, collaboration, and being part of a group. Social media allow teens to extend their personal interactions beyond physical boundaries. So conversations and interactions that begin in person do not have to end when students go their separate ways. They are in constant communication with one another day and night. In fact, kids today appear to be more available to their devices and their social networks than they are to their families.

Shifting the focus slightly to another trend, the digital generations play more than 230 hours of video games a month, or 10,000 hours of gaming by the time they're twenty-one years old. Consider that 10,000 hours of gaming is about 24 hours less than they spend in a classroom for all of intermediate and high school if they have perfect attendance. Many gamers spend more than 40 hours a week playing games, which is the equivalent of a full-time job (McGonigal, 2011b). Once again, in case you think gaming is just a guy thing, it's not. The fastest-growing sector of the mobile gaming market is women between the ages of eight and twenty-five using smart-phones or tablets. In fact, 52 percent of all gamers are women. Increasingly, women are hooked on gaming too (Jayanth, 2014).

Let's switch to video. Video is becoming the preferred channel of communication. Internet video accounted for 40 percent of all Internet traffic in 2012. By 2016, it's expected that number will jump to 62 percent (Cisco, 2014b). As of June 2014, every 60 seconds—24 hours a day—more than 500,000 videos are being viewed on

YouTube (Schaaf & Mohan, 2014). That's almost 5 billion YouTube views a day—or almost 2 trillion playbacks in the last year. Two trillion playbacks is roughly 170 video views for every person on the planet. The amount of video being uploaded to YouTube is almost beyond imagination. Every minute of every day, 24 hours a day, 365 days a year, 100 hours of new video are uploaded. That's 4 days' worth of video uploaded every minute, 24 hours a day. In other words, every minute, viewers are another 4 days behind in their viewing. Consider that 100 hours a minute is almost 6,500 years of content uploaded every year.

Now let's talk about Facebook. There are more than 22 billion visits to Facebook monthly (Smith, 2015). Facebook and all the other social networking tools encourage interaction with the digital world, rather than just passive consumption of online materials. Social media like Facebook give people a soapbox from which to express their opinions.

Every 60 seconds on Facebook, users send 230,000 messages, update 95,000 statuses, write 80,000 wall posts, take 65,000 photos, share 50,000 links, and make 500,000 comments (Fast Company, 2014). Of teens, 79 percent reach for their smartphones within fifteen minutes of waking up (Murphy, 2013). They use these devices to connect to their culture. The use of social media is not optional for kids today. For them, the world is just one great big social network. Today's digital generations expect, in fact they demand, immediate feedback from social networks, video games, and dozens of other online experiences. School is just one of many nodes on this vast network of personal learning.

And Facebook is just one of many social networking sites. There's Instagram, Twitter, Snapchat, Edmodo, Reddit, Tumblr, Tinder . . . the ever-changing list goes on and on! It's a real challenge to keep current on the latest tools and their statistical significance. It's clear that many of the digital generations, as well as older people, are completely consumed by social media.

"How consumed?" you might ask. A Cisco survey of teens reports that one in three indicate that the Internet is as important as air, shelter, food, and water sources. Meanwhile 60 percent of those surveyed in China and Brazil believe that the Internet is *more* important than air, shelter, food, and water sources (Cisco, 2012a).

Many of the older generations interpret this fascination with social networking by the digital generations as addiction to their technologies. As danah boyd (2014), author of *It's Complicated*, points out, what appears from the outside to be addiction to technology is in fact addiction to friendship—friendship that is a hybrid mix of online and face-to-face interactions. The digital generations view the technologies as simply the portals to this friendship.

So What's Going On?

Why are the digital generations spending so much time with their digital technology, and why is the amount of time spent using these technologies increasing so quickly? There are many reasons why this is happening. The Internet is a telephone, television, game console, and radio seamlessly wrapped up into one device. Teens go online to chat with their friends, kill boredom, experience the wider world, and follow the latest trends. They use their devices to meet, play, date, and learn. The Internet is an integral part of their social life. It's how they acknowledge each other and form their personal identities.

For many of the digital generations, exposure to this new digital landscape may be the first experience in their lives with empowerment. Digital technologies enable them to be heard, recognized, and taken seriously. Social media such as Twitter and Facebook are not just about casual commentary, online socializing, or passive consumption of digital information. Social media encourages interaction in and with the digital world, providing both individuals and groups with a platform from which to express personal and collective perspectives, opinions, and contributions about every imaginable topic.

Gary's Social Media Count (Hayes, n.d.) is a website that summarizes data from hundreds of online sources and sites and updates on a second-by-second basis what's happening in the new digital landscape. It shows activities such as the number of new members of Facebook, the number of tablets and smartphones sold, the number of tweets sent, the number of apps downloaded, the number of games played, the number of Skype phone calls made, the number of Google searches, the number of photos added to Flickr, the number of craigslist ads created, and so on. We recommend you take a moment to look at the site. The numbers being generated are absolutely staggering. And as you watch the numbers relentlessly grow in real time, you need to be reminded that this is happening 24 hours a day, 365 days a year. That's digital bombardment!

The problem is, after a while, the numbers become meaningless. So let's pause for a moment and ask again, "What's going on here?" Why are the digital generations spending so much time with their digital technologies? And why is this amount of time spent using digital resources increasing so rapidly?

What we want you to take away from this chapter is that what we're experiencing isn't just a passing fad that's here today and gone tomorrow. Digital culture is the new normal—not just locally, regionally, or nationally, but worldwide. This new world of digital immersion has affected virtually every aspect of our lives, from our thought processes and work habits, to our capacity for linear thinking, to how we feel about ourselves, our friends, and even distant strangers. And this has all happened virtually overnight.

Even though each of the authors of this book has on occasion been accused of being a master of hyperbole, it's almost impossible to overstate the significance of what's happening right now. This new digital landscape is not a temporary aberration. It represents a fundamental and, we believe, irreversible shift in the way we communicate.

If you haven't adopted social media in a significant way, you run the risk of shutting out the most powerful communications channel ever known, and this is just the beginning. We're still very early on in the social networking revolution. As parents, citizens, and particularly educators, we have no choice but to engage with this new digital reality and work to ensure that it affects our children in healthy and responsible ways.

The Challenges of Digital Bombardment and Our Approach

What we have just described is what we have been referring to as we talk about digital bombardment. This is the pervasive influence of digital exposure today on the lives of children and adults alike. The greatest challenge we face at this time is that our generations are struggling as they try to understand the new digital landscape, because almost none of the things described in this chapter are experiences that we had when we were growing up.

So let's cut to the chase: from our personal observations, here's what we understand about the digital generations. We will start by summarizing what we know about digital learners' learning styles and learning preferences. Then we will compare those learning styles and learning preferences to the traditional teaching styles and teaching preferences that continue to be used in many classrooms. We will next briefly discuss what these differences mean in terms of teaching, learning, and assessment of that learning. Then we will identify specific tools and strategies that can be used to appeal to the learning styles and learning preferences of the digital generations. Finally, we will pose critical questions to reflect on.

The digital generations share a common global culture that is defined not entirely by age, but also by how they interact with digital technologies, information, and one another. Whether it is teachers or administrators or parents or school district staff or school board members or people at the department of education or state and provincial politicians—very few adults have had any real long-term exposure to the digitally infused life experiences of the students who populate our schools. The simple truth is that the majority of the adults responsible for engaging students with their instruction have had little experience with the way kids are living their lives today, and so they are out of touch. As a result, there is a growing gap between how the digital generations and how older generations view the world.

Having said that, it's important for us to stress that the attributes we will describe don't apply equally to every learner in every location. There are clearly a range of behaviors that are affected by factors such as culture, socioeconomics, geography, and personal experiences. Over the course of the past several years, we have traveled to the richest and poorest regions of the world, including North America, Europe, the Far East, Australasia, the Middle East, the Indian subcontinent, Africa, and South America—and what we're about to describe here we have seen just about everywhere.

Summarizing the Main Points

This section provides readers with a recap of important information covered in the chapter.

- Outwardly, today's children look the same as we did in the past, but neurologically they are quite different from the older generations.

- Digital bombardment—the pervasive exposure to digital technology —is literally wiring and rewiring kids' brains on an ongoing basis.

- Researchers have determined that children process information in a fundamentally different manner than older generations.

- As parents, citizens, and educators, we must engage with the digital generations and their new digital reality so that they can use digital tools and media in a healthy, responsible manner.

- The digital generations have specific learning attributes that impact teaching, learning, and assessment in today's classrooms; educators can use specific tools and strategies to appeal to the learning preferences of digital learners.

Questions to Consider

Now that you've finished the chapter, consider the following questions.

1. Look back at the extensive statistics in the chapter. What's your response to these numbers?

2. Do you think digital bombardment has any impact on the way the digital generations think? Does it have any impact on the way they learn? Does it have any impact on the way they view the world? Do you think it has any impact on what interests and engages them?

3. In your opinion, why do the members of the digital generations flock to use technology and social media?

4. What will be the consequences, today and in the future, if educators ignore the digital generations' learning preferences?

5. What is the digital divide? How does the digital divide affect the growing gap between the haves and have-nots, and the knows and know-nots?

For up-to-date resource materials
related to this chapter, please visit
http://bit.ly/Attributes_of_Digital_Learners.

Chapter 4

A Need for Speed

The Internet is the most important single development in the history of human communication since the invention of call waiting.

—Dave Barry

Learning Attribute 1

Digital learners prefer receiving information quickly from multiple, hyperlinked digital sources. The traditional educational approach involves a slow and controlled release of information from limited, nondigital sources.

While it's probably not a big surprise, let us explain the enormous implications of this. Digital learners have spent their entire lives operating at twitch speed and suffer from FOMO—Fear of Missing Out. According to Larry Rosen (2010), three-quarters of teens and young adults check their devices every fifteen minutes or less, and if not allowed to do so, they become highly anxious. Many of them—and many of us—can't get through a day without constantly scanning, texting, calling, tweeting, or logging into a digital world that has become so deeply embedded in our lives that living without it seems almost impossible.

As a result, many people today—young and old alike—suffer from AOADD—Always On Attention Deficit Disorder. Many kids arrive at kindergarten with a fast-food mentality and an expectation for instant access, instant gratification, instant feedback, instant recognition, instant success, and instant change. This death of patience—the need to constantly be connected—is primarily due to their lifelong exposure to video games, handheld devices, smartphones, hypertext, and all of the other aspects of our increasingly digital, high-paced world. Because of chronic digital bombardment, the digital generations have had a great deal more experience processing information at a far faster rate than we have. So naturally, they're much better at dealing with high-speed information than older generations are. They have fast-twitch wiring—digital is their native language, and instant gratification is their way of life. It's the way they grew up. Their world has always been this way.

The challenge that many traditional educators face is that they haven't had the same kind of online, high-speed experiences that their students have. As a result, it's completely understandable that many traditional teachers feel comfortable only when they're processing information at the conventional speeds they've experienced most of their lives. Consequently, they don't always understand or appreciate the digital generations' chronic need for speed.

Digital learners spend hundreds, if not thousands, of hours of their lives before and after school and on weekends and holidays playing video games, surfing the web, wandering around in virtual environments, and using their smartphones, tablets, or other digital devices. Then they come to school, where many of them tell us that they feel like they've run into a wall when they're confronted by the awesome technological power of an overhead projector or dry-erase board.

In many cases, the technology and available resources in their home or in their pocket are more powerful than what's available to them at school. So, from the perspective of the digital generations, many teachers and schools unconsciously slam on the brakes. We've had kids regularly tell us that they feel like they have to dumb it down and slow it down when they walk into the classroom. They feel like they've been fed some kind of powerful sedative.

Imagine students as they leave the outside world and enter the classroom. Outside of school, they're interacting with friends, using social media on smartphones and iPads, listening to playlists of music that they've downloaded from the Internet, or making and sharing videos on YouTube. Meanwhile, at school, they get to carry around heavy backpacks of books and listen to teachers reading off the board and talking at them while they take notes using a pen and paper. Can there be a more stark contrast between the two halves of their lives? They're in the 21st century when they're at home and in the community, and they're in the 20th century at school. At home they power up. At school they have to power down.

Kids tell us that when they walk into a classroom for the first time, whether teachers realize it or not, the teachers are on the clock. They tell us that the teacher has fifteen minutes or less to prove two things to them: first, that the teacher gets it—that teachers understand digital culture or are at least trying to—and second, that they respect the students and their world. If the students sense the teacher gets it, a bond of mutual respect is formed. But if they sense the teacher doesn't get it and doesn't respect them or their world, they won't just sit there passively. They will actively work to undermine the teacher.

If we want to really connect with the digital generations, we need to start by acknowledging the absolute centrality of digital culture in their lives, and we need to be willing, at least part of the time, to acknowledge, accept, embrace, and show respect for the digital world that is an everyday and internalized part of their lives. To do this, we must meet them where they are, taking the time necessary to rethink our roles so that students don't have to radically repackage what they learn in school to make it relevant to their personal lives.

But that's part of the ongoing problem we've been encountering in education. Throughout history, educators have regularly struggled and resisted trying to come to terms with new innovations and tools that are central to society, only to change their minds later—typically much later—when the educational value of the new innovations and tools finally becomes clear.

Father Stanley Bezuska of Boston College provided several examples (whether they are real or fictitious is open to debate) from throughout history of the struggle to understand and integrate new technologies into education as told in David Thornburg's (1992) book *Edutrends 2010: Restructuring, Technology, and the Future of Education*:

- At a teacher's conference in 1703 it was reported that students could no longer prepare bark to calculate problems. They depended instead on expensive slates. What would students do when the slates were dropped and broken?

- In 1815, it was reported at a principals' meeting that students depended too much on paper and no longer knew how to write on a slate without getting dust all over themselves. What would happen when they ran out of paper?

- The National Association of Teachers reported in 1907 that students depended too much on ink and no longer knew how to use a knife to sharpen a pencil.

- According to the Rural American Teacher in 1928, students depended too much on store-bought ink. They did not know how to make their own. They wouldn't be able to write until their next trip to the settlement.

- In 1950, it was observed that ballpoint pens would be the ruin of education. Students were using these devices, and then just throwing them away. The values of thrift and frugality were being discarded. Businesses and banks would never allow such expensive luxuries. (pp. 58–59)

In keeping with the spirit of Father Bezuska's list, there are also additional examples of new technologies struggling for acceptance in education (Thornburg, 1992).

- In 1966, it was noted that electronic calculators would never be able to compete with the computational ability of the human brain.

- In 1988, a speaker at the National Association of Secondary School Principals Conference declared there was no good evidence that most uses of computers significantly improve teaching and learning—and most schools would be better off if they just threw their computers into Dumpsters.

- In 1996, Ian gave his son a laptop to take to school to do research and take notes in preparation for an assignment, and it was immediately confiscated by the teacher.

In retrospect, we can look back at such comments and actions and shake our heads about how shortsighted people can be when dealing with new technological innovations. However, smartphones, tablets, and online social networking tools such as Instagram, Twitter, Skype, Snapchat, YouTube, Facebook, cloud-based apps, and file sharing, not to mention Wikipedia and blogs, are just some of the latest technologies to be thrown under the bus by education. The crazy thing is that this is happening at the same time as almost every student is carrying a personal and powerful network in his or her pocket.

The National Association of State Boards of Education (2012), one of the most conservative educational organizations in the United States, released a report called *Born in Another Time: Ensuring Educational Technology Meets the Needs of Students Today—and Tomorrow*, which suggests that schools could no longer be the last place to catch up to the present.

Adults continue to debate whether students deserve the right to learn with the very same tools that the adults rely on for success every day. School is one of the only places where kids can't regularly pull out a device to answer questions. In the process, students are being left unprepared for their futures.

National Association of State Boards of Education (2012) states that schools must catch up to students and not the other way around. They suggest that students need to be using smartphones, iPads, and other personal digital devices as academic tools for research and learning, the same way students use Bunsen burners or microscopes. Particularly in times of budgetary shortfalls, it's absolutely foolish not to allow students to use these devices in schools for educational purposes. Rather than banning these devices from classrooms, we should be showing students how to use them appropriately.

Kids are regularly given smartphones and Internet access with little guidance as to how to use them responsibly. Then when they inevitably do foolish things as many of them do, adults shake their heads and use that as justification for banning these devices from the classroom. We wouldn't give a kid the keys to a car without first teaching him how to drive, making sure he had a license, and making it clear that he had to be home by 10 p.m., that he was not allowed to drink and drive, and that there would be consequences if he did stupid things. In the same way, students need to be given clear boundaries as to the appropriate use of, and behavior with, digital technologies.

When schools ignore or reject the technologies and online world that are happening almost everywhere outside of schools, and when schools ban students from using digital devices and online resources, the hidden message we send to students is that schools are decades behind and completely disengaged from the very population they're supposed to be working with. Instead of blocking the use of these devices, maybe education should acknowledge that it's time to meet the digital generations in their own space and show them how to appropriately use their preferred technologies to engage in classroom learning.

When we try to ban the devices and resources that are an everyday part of the lives of young and old alike, whether it's at school or work or home, without first carefully considering the educational possibilities and potential of these devices, we're absolutely blowing an opportunity to connect with and engage the digital generations—and in doing so, we run the risk of losing them.

Put simply, the message to educators is this: the world has changed—it's time for us to acknowledge it. It's time for us to get over it and get on with adequately preparing our students for the world that awaits them once they leave school, not just preparing them for the world we experienced when we were growing up.

The world that digital learners live in today includes one of the greatest collections in human history—the Internet. Students are able to access billions of interconnected webpages and resources and use them to construct their own knowledge. However, to effectively use the power of the Internet, students and teachers alike must be able to distinguish between the flash and substance of online resources.

Strategies and Tools That Work

What follows are some examples of learning strategies and web-based tools that help address digital learners' desire to receive information quickly from multiple, hyperlinked digital sources.

Wikipedia: www.wikipedia.org

Wikipedia is a multilingual, collaboratively edited, free online encyclopedia that contains over 30 million articles in 287 languages. Due to large-scale editing by numerous, unverified sources, Wikipedia has been dismissed by many as an unreliable, untrustworthy resource. However, it is one of the most used sources of information on the web. As someone searches a term using Google, Yahoo, or Bing, a Wikipedia entry is often one of the first resources fetched by search engines.

Should Wikipedia entries be trusted? The answer is yes and no. Wikipedia is a wonderful tool for starting the research process. Each entry is organized and categorized into relevant subheadings, and important vocabulary terms are linked to other Wikipedia articles to allow readers to investigate the subject in greater depth.

For example, if a reader is researching Newton's first law of relativity, she can quickly access the page on "Forces" to gain background information on the term and definition. (See figure 4.1.)

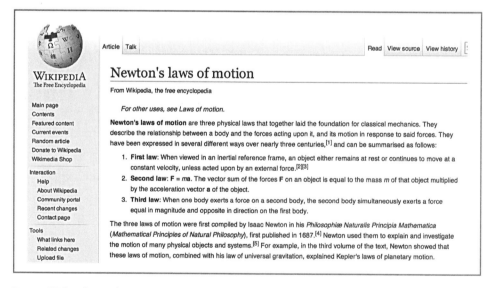

Source: Wikipedia, n.d.

Figure 4.1: Wikipedia entry for Newton's law of motion.

Wikipedia isn't impervious to misinformation. Practically anyone can edit a Wikipedia entry. Although it has content editors, there aren't nearly enough to check every single Wikipedia edit. The collective efforts of everyone involved with the constant updates and edits completed daily are hard to imagine. To get a sense of the scale and scope of Wikipedia, visit http://en.wikipedia.org/wiki/Wikipedia:Statistics#Edits (Wikipedia: Statistics, n.d.) for up-to-date statistics.

Wikipedia articles can be open to bias, misinformation, vandalism, and simple mistakes. However, a 2005 study completed by *Nature* magazine compared the information accuracy of Encyclopedia Britannica and Wikipedia. The results found "the difference in accuracy was not particularly great: the average science entry in Wikipedia contained around four inaccuracies; Britannica, about three" (Giles, 2005).

To be clear, Wikipedia should never be used as the final source or solution for research. Rather, it must be considered as a starting point for any research journey. Whether it is on Wikipedia or any other source, students must learn how to analyze, triangulate, and authenticate the information they find.

Students can:

- Read articles associated with a topic of interest and search the linking pages to develop background knowledge

- Use the subheadings to mind-map during the research process

- Use the reference section to explore supporting or primary sources of information

Google Earth: www.google.com/earth

Google Earth is a virtual globe, map, and geo-information program. It combines satellite and aerial imagery to construct a simulated planet Earth. Over the years, additional features and plug-ins have revolutionized the program, transforming it into a versatile tool for students and teachers alike. (See figure 4.2, page 40.)

Users are able to construct or view 3-D models of buildings and land features, participate in a virtual world tour, visit important landmarks, and click on Wikipedia articles and panoramic views to learn about points and events of interest. The mapping program also includes additional layers to its display such as political borders, location labels, roads, photos, weather, traffic, earthquake locations, volcanic activity, historical mode (to view back in time), and much, much more.

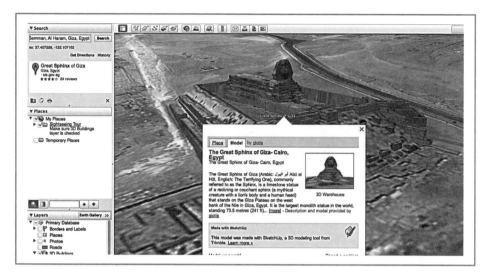

Source: Google, Inc.

Figure 4.2: Google Earth screenshot.

The classroom applications are limitless. For social studies, students have access to accurate satellite photos of Earth with integrated layers of real-world images, Wikipedia links informing viewers on points or events of interest, and cultural and historical resources.

The science applications are also vast and engaging. Students can explore the underwater topography of the oceans, learn about different species of plants and animals, view real-time data on global tremor and volcanic activity, examine weather patterns and phenomena, and track tagged marine life.

In literature, readers can enjoy the cool and immersive Google Lit Trips. Conceptualized by Jerome Burg, these resources are "free downloadable files that mark the journeys of characters from famous literature on the surface of Google Earth. At each location along the journey there are placemarks with pop-up windows containing a variety of resources including relevant media, thought-provoking discussion starters, and links to supplementary information about 'real world' references made in that particular portion of the story" (GLT Global ED, n.d.). Google Lit Trips are constructed not to replace traditional reading assignments, but rather to enhance them with rich, robust media resources that encourage higher-order thinking skills and real-world connectivity. Some of these exciting literature trips include *The Grapes of Wrath*, *Number the Stars*, *The Odyssey*, and *Make Way for Ducklings*. Another wonderful approach would be to flip the learning and have students create their own Lit Trips.

Google Earth is a free download available at the Apple App Store, from Google Play, or for computer download.

eBooks

eBooks aren't just digital copies based on traditional books. Many are now hyperlinked road maps to a multilayered reading and viewing experience. In traditional books, if a new word or concept challenges a reader, the reader has to stop and research the word or skip it and lose out on a potential learning experience. With an eBook, readers have their choice to read the text from beginning to end as in traditional books or read in a nonlinear fashion by stopping, performing deeper research and reflection, then returning to the text where they left off.

eBooks can contain the same types of hyperlinks as a webpage with links to valuable resources for readers to explore and study. Websites, videos, blogs, reference pages, and images are just some of the resources found on the other end of a link. The presentation of an eBook is also vastly different, containing interactive images, 3-D models, embedded video, audio clips, collaborative discussion forums, and interactive galleries and slide shows alongside the text.

Moreover, when content changes over time, an eBook can be quickly updated without incurring the large expense needed to replace costly, paper-based textbooks.

With web connectivity, eBooks can provide readers with truly unique reading and learning experiences that can benefit all content areas.

Aggregators

Aggregators are web programs or computer software that aggregates or collects specific types of information from multiple online sources. They have been around for many years, but with the evolution of social media, content has become much easier to share with others. Instead of the traditional method of searching for content using a search engine, aggregators fetch, filter, and organize results using criteria set by the user.

Scoop.it is a topic-centered content curation app or service that allows users to identify a topic, find content using smart searches or the Scoop.it community, collect and add the curator's own perspective to the content, and share using social media utilities. For example, if a user identifies "robots" as a central, curated theme, then hundreds of resources are provided for the user to explore and organize. In addition, other users can post comments, make suggestions, or add other meaningful resources using the collaborative power of the web. (See figure 4.3, page 42.)

Figure 4.3: Scoop.it screenshot.

Any subject in school that requires research and collaboration will benefit from the use of an aggregator, allowing students to spend less time searching and more time curating, collaborating, and making connections from what they have read to the learning topic.

A Google a Day: www.agoogleaday.com

With more and more of the world's content online, it is critical that students understand how to effectively use search techniques to find quality sources appropriate to their task. Google has created a fun and engaging way for teachers to guide students using search strategies meaningfully in their academics. A Google a Day offers challenging topics for students to research each day. Students are asked to search and locate the answers to questions in subjects such as culture, geography, history, and science. The site also contains literacy lessons to help teachers meet the Common Core State Standards. They are categorized based on beginner, intermediate, or advanced levels of expertise in searching.

Using A Google a Day is a wonderful warm-up strategy for engaging students in meaningful, student-centered tasks. The various subject areas and topics of the search questions vary from day to day, so this project could potentially lead into more extensive research projects and presentations. The site also offers badges and points for intrinsic incentives to entice students to do their best during the challenges. (See figure 4.4 for an example of A Google a Day.)

Source: Google, Inc.

Figure 4.4: A Google a Day screenshot.

Additional Strategies, Apps, and Resources to Explore

What follows is a section with more strategies, apps, and resources to consider using with the always-on generation.

WebQuest: http://webquest.org

Developed by Bernie Dodge, WebQuests are inquiry-oriented lessons where most or all of the information that learners work with comes from the web. Learners are introduced to tasks they must accomplish and have their work evaluated based on set criteria.

*Hyperlink Lane: www.infosavvy21.com/blog/2014/9/18
/hyperlink-lane-creating-a-web-map-for-learner-research*

Facilitators locate web resources for their learners during a research or exploratory activity and list hyperlinks in a logical or sequential order. The list of links becomes a map for the learner to explore and examine. Teachers take away some of the guess-work for the learner by providing prescreened, high-quality content for students to explore.

Flipboard: https://flipboard.com

Flipboard collects and curates web content into a stylish, easy-to-read, personalized digital magazine on the web or mobile devices. You can also create and share your own magazine with others. Flipboard is available from Apple's App Store and Google Play.

Feedly: http://feedly.com/i/welcome

Similar to Flipboard, Feedly is an impressive aggregator that compiles new feeds from numerous online sources and displays them on a personalized homepage for the reader.

WolframAlpha: www.wolframalpha.com

WolframAlpha uses mathematical computation and factual data to calculate answers. Differing from a search engine that hunts and retrieves webpages and documents with potential answers to queries, WolframAlpha attempts to answer the question directly. For example, How long is the Great Wall of China? In a matter of seconds, WolframAlpha identifies its length in standard and metric units (13,171 miles or 21,196 kilometers). Users can also ask questions related to mathematics, linguistics, culture, astronomy, engineering, and dozens of other subjects.

Summarizing the Main Points

This section provides readers with a recap of important information covered in the chapter.

- Digital learners prefer receiving information quickly from multiple, hyperlinked digital sources.
- The traditional educational approach involves a slow and controlled release of information from limited, nondigital sources.

- Because of chronic digital bombardment, the digital generations have far more experience at processing information at a far faster rate than members of the older generations do.

- If educators want to connect with the digital generations, they must start by acknowledging the absolute centrality of digital culture in the digital generations' lives and embrace the digital world that is an everyday and internalized part of their lives.

- The National Association of State Boards of Education states that schools must catch up to students and not the other way around.

Questions to Consider

Now that you've finished the chapter, consider the following questions.

1. What happens to engagement and learning when you have students who operate at twitch speed and a teacher who doesn't?

2. Why is it critical to teach digital learners how to use digital tools efficiently and ethically?

3. Why will banning digital tools and social media in the classroom be detrimental for the digital generations?

4. What happens when an educator embracing the digital tools of the digital generations is in the classroom for 21st century teaching, learning, and assessment?

5. Why does education regularly struggle to adopt new innovations and tools that are central to society?

For up-to-date resource materials
related to this chapter, please visit
http://bit.ly/Attributes_of_Digital_Learners.

Chapter 5

The Multitasking Mind

You can do two things at once, but you can't
focus effectively on two things at once.

—GARY KELLER

Learning Attribute 2

Digital learners prefer parallel processing and multitasking. Traditional models of teaching promote linear processing and single or limited tasks.

There have been great concerns expressed about the inability of the digital generations to follow long and complex arguments. The rapid access, skim-and-leave reading behavior fostered by surfing the Internet, coupled with the multitasking mindset that is common in the digital world today, has made the digital generations less likely to work their way through documents that require a patient approach to follow longer, more challenging thoughts, opinions, and arguments.

From the very earliest of times, people have always been able to multitask. Technically, it's called *continuous partial attention*—where we randomly switch between tasks, deciding which one to do next, and time-slice our attention. We do it every day. We're driving in the car, listening to music, sipping on some water, thinking about what happened at work today, considering what to do tonight, and reading a billboard, seemingly all at the same time.

But with the digital generations, this multitasking all happens much faster. There is so much going on. The digital generations are sending text messages, watching Internet videos, listening to downloaded playlists of music, talking on smartphones, looking at brightly colored flashing websites, sending instant messages, and generally counting on the Internet as their external brain. As a result, their minds must continually skim and skip between tasks to keep up. This butterfly brain effect can be a real challenge when educators are trying to get students to focus on important tasks or employers are trying to get workers to focus on their jobs.

What the research says is that effective multitasking is really about having a good memory, capable of being able to pay attention to several *familiar* tasks at one time, while also being highly adept at task-switching. This isn't the way the older generations grew up. This is not what most of us experienced as children.

Ian personally remembers his father coming into his bedroom and telling him to turn off his radio because he was supposed to be studying for a test—that listening to music was a distraction. He told Ian that the best way to study was to isolate himself from the TV, tape player, and busy sidewalk outside Ian's bedroom window. Ian's father told him what he needed to do was clear a nice, uncluttered study space with a comfy chair, good lighting, and ample working area.

Compare that approach and traditional mindset to the way that the digital generations function today. How many of you have walked into a kid's bedroom recently? There our students are, working on a tablet, earbuds dangling around their neck cranking out the music of some band you've never heard of before, their hand reflexively tapping to the backbeat of the song. Meanwhile, they're also doing their homework, watching a YouTube video, tweeting a friend, downloading some music and an image from Google, and cybershopping, while they're simultaneously carrying on two conversations on Instagram about last night's concert—and another screen holds an old Pong game paused in mid-ping. And if you ask them, they'll tell you they're still bored! They'll also tell you they have to play their music loud because it helps them concentrate—something that many of the older generations simply can't fathom.

In his book *Brain Rules*, John Medina (2008) tells us that research on multitasking indicates that contrary to what the digital generations might believe, multitasking modern students are not nearly as effective at concentrating on a particular task as those who single task. In fact, humans are biologically incapable of processing multiple information-rich inputs simultaneously. Medina says that the effect of multitasking on productivity is like trying to get something done after you've had several stiff drinks. We might *think* we are doing very well, but in reality we're slower and sloppier, and we make many more mistakes. His studies show clearly that someone who is regularly interrupted takes 50 percent longer to complete a task and makes up to 50 percent more errors.

In *iBrain*, Gary Small and Gigi Vorgan (2008) point out that while multitasking is an essential skill in the digital world, to minimize the negative aspects of doing multiple tasks simultaneously, we must balance multitasking with strategies for developing single-tasking skills: "Multitasking has become a necessary skill of modern life, but we need to acknowledge the challenges and adapt accordingly. Several strategies can help, such as striving to stay on one task longer, and avoiding task switching whenever possible" (p. 69).

It's absolutely critical that we help all of our students understand that there are other essential metacognitive skills beyond being able to multitask that they will all need to learn—and that they need to learn how to focus on single tasks for extended periods of time. But this is not a matter of either/or. At the same time that students need to learn how to focus for extended periods of time, they also need to know how to effectively switch their attention between multiple tasks or technologies.

In *Brain Rules*, Medina (2008) says that educators need to acknowledge that multimedia multitasking is an everyday reality of life—that students do not suffer notable cognitive shortcomings as they multitask; rather, they are learning more, and they are more adept at finding answers to deep questions, in part because they can search effectively and access collective intelligence. And Medina cautions that the solution to the challenges of multitasking is not just to remove technology and other distractions, because they are too intricately woven into the digital generations' lives.

The bottom line is that whether we like it or not, and whether we think it was better back then or not, we're never going back to 1985 or even 2005. The problem is that there are parents, politicians, lawmakers, and even some educators who continue to promote an educational model and prepare students for a world that no longer exists.

Strategies and Tools That Work

What follows are some examples of learning strategies and web-based tools that help address digital learners' desire to multitask.

Tech Breaks

In his book *Rewired: Understanding the iGeneration and the Way They Learn*, author Larry Rosen (2010) points out that an emerging trend is students being allowed to use their personal digital devices to do research, take notes, or perform other activities that can promote learning. In such classrooms, teachers often report that students stray off task while using their devices for instructional purposes. This is because the digital generations have a constant urge to check for email and text messages, tweet friends, or access other social media.

Rosen (2010) suggests using a tech break. Tech breaks start with the teacher giving the students one minute to use their personal devices to surf the web or check for tweets, texts, or Snapchat messages. After a minute, the students are expected to turn their device to silent and place them upside down on the corner of their desks and focus on classwork for fifteen minutes. Having their devices upside down prevents external distractions such as vibrations and flashing alerts and provides a signal to the brain that there is no need to be internally distracted, because an opportunity to check again will be coming soon.

At the end of the fifteen-minute focus time, the teacher declares another tech break, and the students take another minute to check in with their virtual worlds, followed by more on-task time and tech breaks. The trick is to gradually lengthen the time between tech breaks to teach students how to focus for longer periods of time without being distracted.

We have seen this technique used successfully by teachers in the classroom, by parents at the dinner table or in a restaurant, and by managers during meetings. Be aware that students are remarkably adept at texting blindly and may put a dummy smartphone on their desk while keeping their primary smartphone in their pocket. Clearly, there have to be consequences if students do not adhere to this program.

Evernote

Evernote is a powerfully versatile app with tremendous potential for personal productivity, research, and collaboration. Evernote offers a basic, free account that includes an abundance of storage space. Unlike most web storage services that offer a set amount of space, Evernote provides a monthly storage allotment of 50 megabytes and resets with each new month. Users create notes similar to a word-processing document and store them online. An Evernote user also has the ability to record audio or video notes, import documents, or enter present mode to create a presentation for viewers. Users can visit their Evernote account online, download software for a Mac or PC, or install apps on mobile devices. Evernote synchronizes the notes to web storage, making notes available across all devices. (See figure 5.1.)

Evernote Web Clipper is a web browser extension available for Google Chrome, Mozilla Firefox, and Safari. If a user stumbles upon a valuable online resource such as a webpage, blog, or article, she can click an icon and import the resource with active links, images, and text into her account. The web is a volatile environment with webpages appearing and disappearing on a regular basis. Using Evernote to upload web content helps teachers secure valuable resources and curate them for students for instruction.

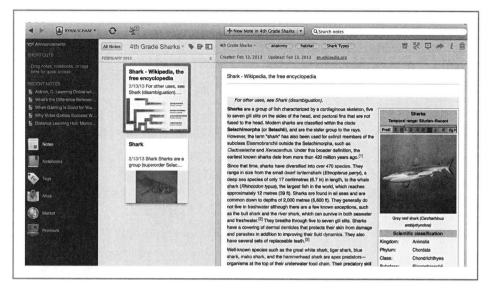

Source: Used under license from Evernote Corporation.

Figure 5.1: Evernote screenshot.

Older students can collect articles they find online while maintaining the links incorporated throughout the text for their research needs, use Evernote as a functional word processor, curate content in a portfolio, take or record notes, present, store files, construct mind maps, and share with their classmates while using whatever device they have in their possession. This app was tailor made for multitaskers.

Socrative

Socrative is a smart student response system that empowers teachers to engage their students through a series of educational exercises and games utilizing smartphones, laptops, and tablets. In a matter of minutes, teachers can set up an interactive activity and capture authentic attitudinal or performance data from their students. Since Socrative is free and available on all digital platforms, students are able to select the device they wish to use during learning activities.

Socrative is a versatile assessment tool that can be utilized in all content areas. Teachers can use it to create a warm-up activity to gauge prior experiences, develop a gaming experience using one of several activity choices offered when building an activity, or create an exit ticket with the ability to view real-time data to determine future instruction for students. (See figure 5.2, page 52.)

Source: Socrative. Used with permission.

Figure 5.2: Socrative on multiple devices screenshot.

Speech-to-Text Software

Digital devices and software have evolved to the point where voice recognition is exceptionally accurate and intuitive. With Apple's release of its digital personal assistant, Siri, more and more people are using a new means to search for information without typing on a keyboard. The same ability also exists to speak words to a screen. Software such as Dragon® Dictate has been around for years, but with each new release, the software becomes more accurate and easier to use. With an incredible 99 percent accuracy and a short five-minute training session, humans and computers no longer need the tap, tap, tapping of a keyboard. Teachers can easily reduce the amount of time it takes to answer emails, type notes, give feedback to students, or capture important information for students who are absent or have learning challenges.

For students, speech-to-text software allows them to multitask. Students can record notes while they are reading and searching for relevant content during the research process. They can also give themselves spoken reminders such as homework assignments, ideas generated through oral brainstorming, or starting the rough draft to a blog post or creative writing assignment.

Google Forms

Different Google Apps will be showcased extensively throughout the book, but the power of Google Forms easily lends itself to student and teacher multitasking. With Google Drive, which is available on all digital devices, users have the ability to create forms and easily collect information. Users can create new forms and build surveys with empty fields or multiple types of questions for visitors to enter information in. Question types include multiple choice, short text, paragraph text, checkboxes, and choose from a list, date, time, scale, and grid. In conjunction with Google Drive, the form builder can include page breaks, section headers, images, and even video.

When the visitor inputs information into the form, it automatically populates a Google spreadsheet in real time. The provider of the form has the ability to share a link, invite people over social networks, or embed the form on a webpage. The user can view results as they stream in from visitors, download the form results as a spreadsheet or PDF, or even display item results in graph form.

Google Forms is easily a teacher's best friend. It would be difficult to think of a school subject that would not benefit from its use. Teachers are able to create warm-ups to activate student thinking at the beginning of a lesson, forego the need for the dreaded worksheet, and use forms to collect activity responses, hold tests and quizzes online, or develop an exit ticket for real-time lesson closure and analysis. Outside of instruction, teachers may use it to collect information from parents, students, and staff members.

Students can use it to collect their own data during a math or science class. Outside of class, students can collect community information, develop petitions, survey the student body, or address any other matter where open (or even anonymous) data collection is necessary. (See figure 5.3, page 54.)

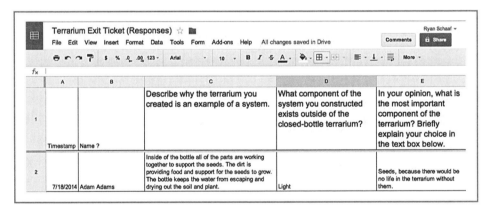

Source: Google, Inc.

Figure 5.3: An example of a Google Form and the spreadsheet it populates.

Additional Strategies, Apps, and Resources to Explore

What follows is a section with more strategies, apps, and resources to consider using with the always-on generation.

Screencasts

Screencasts are used to develop video tutorials that demonstrate actions or processes occurring on a screen, including the ability to create audio narrations describing what the user is doing. This can easily be used by teachers to demonstrate a new concept or skill or by students to produce a multimedia project. Mobile devices such as smartphones and tablets have their own apps for screencasts. Some screencast tools include:

- Explain Everything (Apple and Droid)—https://itunes.apple.com/us/app /explain-everything/id431493086?mt=8

- ShowMe (Apple)—https://itunes.apple.com/us/app/showme-interactive -whiteboard/id445066279?mt=8

- Screenr (web based)—www.screenr.com

- Screencast-O-Matic (web based)—www.screencast-o-matic.com

- Jing (Windows or Mac)—www.techsmith.com/jing.html

Digital Timers

Digital timers are a simple but effective method for rationing instructional time. They are simply apps or utilities that track time or act as a visual stopwatch. The following lists several different web-based digital timers. Mobile devices such as smartphones and tablets have clock apps with these features (see figure 5.4.).

- www.online-stopwatch.com/full-screen-stopwatch

- http://timer.onlineclock.net

- http://e.ggtimer.com

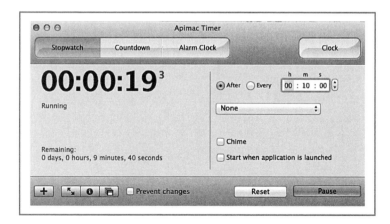

Source: Apimac. Used with permission.

Figure 5.4: Apimac digital timer interface screenshot.

Dropbox: www.dropbox.com/login?lhs_type=anywhere

Dropbox is an online file-hosting service that allows users to easily store, access, share, or synchronize files or folders using email and social networks, or access hyperlinks via a computer, tablet, or smartphone.

SymbalooEDU: www.symbalooedu.com

SymbalooEDU is a bookmark homepage that quickly memorizes your favorite websites and organizes them in one place.

Summarizing the Main Points

This section provides readers with a recap of important information covered in the chapter.

- There is great debate as to whether or not the digital generations have the attention span to read extensive texts or follow long and complex arguments.

- Humans can perform multiple, familiar tasks simultaneously, but unfamiliar tasks are often completed slower and with more errors.

- Despite what the older generations might believe, digital learners don't suffer notable cognitive shortcomings as they multitask.

- As important as multitasking is to the digital generations, they must also be able to focus for extended periods of time on single tasks.

- Many parents, politicians, policymakers, and even some educators continue to promote an educational model that prepares students for a world that no longer exists.

- Students must use tools that are constructed and designed to cater to their propensity for multitasking.

Questions to Consider

Now that you've finished the chapter, consider the following questions.

1. What does research suggest about improving the ability to multitask?

2. How does digital learners' preference to work differ from our parents' mindset of completing homework?

3.   What advice does John Medina offer when dealing with a multitasking digital learner?

4.   What types of learning activities can educators utilize with students to take advantage of collective intelligence?

5.   How can teachers promote students' multitasking preferences and at the same time encourage them to remain focused on single tasks for longer periods of time?

For up-to-date resource materials
related to this chapter, please visit
http://bit.ly/Attributes_of_Digital_Learners.

Chapter 6

EyeWorld

Maybe I'm wrong, but I should say that in ten years textbooks as the principal medium of teaching will be as obsolete as the horse and carriage are now. I believe that in the next ten years, visual education will be a matter of course in all our schools.

—Thomas Edison

Learning Attribute 3

Digital learners prefer processing pictures, sounds, color, and video before they process text. The traditional approach has been to provide students with text before pictures, color, sounds, and video.

For generations, graphics were generally static illustrations, photos, or diagrams that accompanied the text and provided further clarification after the fact. Most of us can remember reading an *Encyclopedia Britannica* or a *Book of Knowledge* when we were children. Back then, the primary information was provided by text, and the images were merely intended to complement the text. But for digital learners, the relationship is almost completely reversed. Increasingly, the role of text is to provide more detail to something that is first experienced as an image or a video.

The members of the always-on generation are growing up in a visual world—a world of the eye. According to John Medina (2008), people can remember the content of more than 2,500 pictures with at least 90 percent accuracy, seventy-two hours after exposure to those images, even though the subjects only see each picture for about ten seconds. One year later, the recall rate for the same 2,500 pictures is still an impressive 63 percent. But the same research says when new information is presented orally with no image present, seventy-two hours later listeners are only able to recall about 10 percent of what is presented.

So what implications does this research hold for today's students? Applying this in a classroom context, seventy-two hours after students have been introduced to content that is combined with images, they would typically be able to recall the content with about 90 percent accuracy; students introduced to the same content without the benefit of images would typically only be able to recall about 10 percent of the content of a lecture.

This is clear evidence that the traditional stand-and-deliver lecture method, where the teacher talks and the students listen (maybe), and where there is no visual component, is just not effective. However, when an image is added to new content after the fact, the percentage retained goes up from 10 percent to 65 percent.

The Power of Color

Another visual factor is the power of color to persuade. Katie Lepi (2014) examines the psychology of the use of color. In business, colors are incorporated into advertising to elicit specific emotional responses. Companies like Coca-Cola, McDonald's, Ford, and Starbucks are masters of using color in their branding to connect with potential customers. The same psychological principles apply in the classroom.

Using colors is an effective way to connect with digital learners. For example, red evokes a feeling of strength, passion, and excitement. However, students often negatively associate the color red with the dreaded marking pen of failure—so the color red has to be used judiciously. Psychologically, the color yellow evokes intellect, joy, energy, fun, and happiness and attracts attention. Blue tends to provoke feelings of loyalty, trust, and intelligence. And green is considered the easiest color for human vision and is often associated with freshness, growth, and safety (Chung, 2014).

A good practice is to carefully consider color choices when making presentations, designing learning materials, creating displays, and communicating with students. It's critical not to underestimate the power of color to inspire and engage learners.

The same considerations apply to the quality of images used in learning materials. Digital learners are very critical consumers when it comes to images. Their eyes quickly distinguish between clip art and photos and between low-quality and high-quality images. It's essential, whenever possible, to avoid stretched or pixelated images and to use photos that are contextual to the topic being explored.

The Visual Generations

Since childhood, the digital generations have been continuously exposed to and bombarded by television, videos, computers, tablets, and video games that put colorful, high-quality, highly expressive, realistic, multisensory experiences—sight, sound, and touch (and likely in the near future smell, taste, and 3-D)—in front of students with little or no accompanying text. As a result, to the digital generations, images and video are powerful enough on their own to communicate messages to and for them. Increasingly for the digital generations, the role of words is simply to complement the images.

We have to keep in mind that these are the first generations in human history that know more about a new innovation that is central to society than the previous generations do. The result of this pervasive and chronic digital bombardment has been to considerably sharpen the digital generations' visual abilities. They are completely comfortable seeing and conveying information in visual formats. And because they were born digital, right before our very eyes, the digital generations are taking control of critical elements of the communications revolution. All you have to do is play a video game against them and get annihilated to realize that their visual-spatial skills are so highly developed that the research seems to indicate that they have cultivated a complete physical interface between digital and real worlds.

Meanwhile, many people of the older generations continue to struggle with trying to understand the fundamental differences between the visual generations and their own, because this is not the world the older generations were born into. Previous generations were paper-trained growing up. They were trained to communicate primarily with words. They were trained to communicate in a linear, logical, left-to-right, top-to-bottom, beginning-to-end manner. Meanwhile, the digital generations are light and sound-trained, which is a completely different cognitive process than the one older generations use.

And the digital generations are not just consuming content; they are simultaneously creating it. They are *transfluent*—they are fluent in a wide range of media. And because they are transfluent, the digital generations find it much more natural than older generations to begin communicating with visuals, and then to mix in text, color, sound, and graphics in richly meaningful and creative ways. They are completely comfortable interacting across a wide range of platforms, tools, and media.

What readers need to take away from this trend is that the digital generations are driving a clear and probably irreversible shift from written media to visual media.

So increasingly for the digital generations, expressing ideas is just as likely to involve creating a simulation or digital mash-up as it would writing an expository essay. They are evolving with their new technologies, so the digital generations will need to be able to communicate as effectively in graphical storytelling modes as older generations were taught to communicate with text.

Strategies and Tools That Work

Adapted from "Visual Discovery in Five Easy Steps" (TCI, 2010)

Today's students live in a visual world. The constant digital bombardment of television shows, YouTube clips, video games, and the Internet has created a visually aware generation. Visual media is an increasing part of their daily viewing diet; however, they're not necessarily critical viewers. In fact, they are far from being visually literate. While on the outside they may appear to be highly sophisticated viewers, in reality many of them are completely overwhelmed by both the quantity and ever-changing nature of visual media.

By helping students learn how to view, interact with, interpret, and analyze visual media, you are helping them develop their visual skills so they can build their own understanding of concepts, perform higher-level thinking, and develop independent problem-solving and analytical skills.

Using Visual Media to Introduce New Concepts

You must acquire powerful examples of visual media that represent the key elements of the lesson. Identifying and using an effective visual prompt becomes the glue that will ensure the concepts stay in the minds of students. Effective visual media:

- Is directly connected to content standards and teaching intentions
- Identifies key ideas, themes, or events in the lesson
- Visually delivers a powerful, emotional message
- Allows students to make a real-world connection

For each visual, ask a series of questions that spiral from basic information ("What did you see?") to critical thinking ("What do you suppose the people are expecting to happen?"). Students often rush to interpret media before carefully inspecting all of the visual details. While their initial interpretations may be accurate, students will come to deeper understandings if they slow down and look for details. There are three stages to the exploration.

First, have students gather evidence. Start by telling them to think of themselves as detectives and to regard what they see as the visuals from a crime scene that they need to investigate. At this level, the task is to scour the crime scene for evidence (TCI, 2010).

Once the evidence has been gathered, have the students interpret the evidence and make inferences based on the existing evidence. As they share their findings, encourage them to discuss their interpretations, together with their supporting evidence. Typical questions at this level are what, when, where, and who (TCI, 2010).

Third, ask the students to make hypotheses from the evidence. At this level, students are asked to use the evidence and their own critical-thinking skills to make hypotheses about what is happening and why. Typically, questions at this level are why and how questions that require higher-order thinking skills such as justifying, synthesizing, predicting, and evaluating (TCI, 2010).

Students Interacting With the Visual Media

An effective teaching strategy for assessing student learning at this early stage is to have students "step up to or into" the visual media to bring it to life. This might include pausing videos and seeking student interpretation of what they have just viewed, analyzing and interpreting how media was used to convey the message, or asking questions about the media and the message.

Tools to Support This Model

The following tools and strategies will take advantage of the always-on generation's affinity for processing visual information.

YouTube: www.youtube.com

YouTube allows billions of people to discover, watch, and share originally created videos. It provides a forum for people to connect, inform, and inspire others across the globe, and acts as a distribution platform for original content creators and advertisers large and small. (See figure 6.1, page 64.)

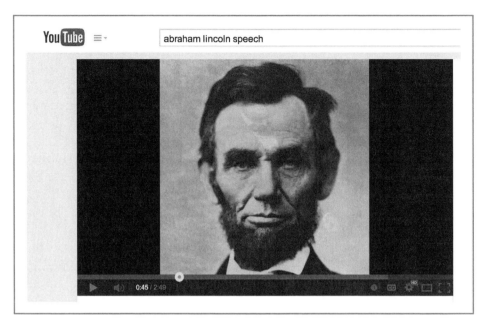

Source: YouTube.

Figure 6.1: YouTube screenshot.

YouTube could be one of the greatest resources for a connected educator. The sheer volume of available videos is staggering. A simple search can retrieve dozens of potential videos to enhance the learning experience for any subject. If a teacher is studying the water cycle, a simple search uncovers thousands of potential video segments to integrate into instruction. If a class is studying Shakespeare, they have access to numerous productions of each of his plays, sonnets, and poems. In social studies, students have access to famous speeches such as Abraham Lincoln's *Gettysburg Address*, Dr. Martin Luther King Jr.'s *I Have a Dream*, Winston Churchill's *We Shall Fight on the Beaches*, and Mahatma Gandhi's *Quit India*. All that is required to leverage the power of YouTube is minimal searching skills and the patience to wade through bad videos to get to the good ones.

For the digital generations, YouTube is perfectly packaged for their consumption. It's visual, social, diverse, mobile, adaptive, and broken down into bite-size chunks in ways that promote engagement and consumption. With more than three hundred hours of new content uploaded every minute and four billion views daily (YouTube, n.d.), YouTube is an amazing video repository of potentially valuable video clips. It's also possible to easily create personal learning channels that can be used for both students and teachers to organize topic-related videos. On a cautionary note, it's absolutely essential for teachers to prescreen all content being considered for use by and with students. Some video clips may be unsuitable or not age-appropriate.

YouTube also provides students with the means to broadcast their content to billions of viewers around the world. Gone are the days of carrying around a camcorder, downloading and editing footage on a computer, and sharing it on a CD or DVD. With the use of smartphones, students can click, record, upload, and share videos in a matter of seconds using their favorite social media outlets.

Instagram: http://instagram.com

Kids today use media to share and socialize. Instagram provides them with the ability to do this in a simple yet eye-catching way. Instagram is an online video- and photo-sharing social network that allows users to take pictures or videos, add visual filters, enhance them by adding special effects, and then share their captured moments with others. It has become an image- and video-sharing powerhouse for the digital generations, with over sixteen billion images and videos shared since its founding and more than 150 million active users (Harris, 2013).

The digital generations are visual beings who covet their mobile devices. Is it any wonder that a free app like Instagram has developed such a powerful and enthusiastic following? The comments section of Instagram also allows viewers to interact with their social networks. But the commenting isn't just commenting—in effect, it's socializing in mixed-media conversations. The possible applications of Instagram, both in and out of the classroom, are almost limitless. During field trips, students can quickly share their experiences with images and videos as well as comment on their own and others' postings. Teachers and chaperones can join the fun and create truly enriching memories for students. Instagram is a simple way to capture images of notes or educational artifacts that might not be otherwise easily copied or transported. By digitizing content, Instagram users can share educational materials in fun ways as easily as they share their selfies or images of their friends. (See figure 6.2, page 66.)

ryanlschaaf
28 seconds ago · ⦿ columbia gym
We caught the big one!

Leave a comment...

Figure 6.2: Instagram screenshot.

VoiceThread: https://voicethread.com

VoiceThread is a cloud-based app that provides users, affectionately referred to as voicethreaders, with the ability to reply to online content using text, audio, and video commentary. Teachers upload documents, presentations, images, audio files, and videos to their VoiceThread account and prepare an instructional activity for students to participate in. Students can conduct reading comprehension of text, engage in peer review of assignments, participate in online discussions and debates, annotate a resource, introduce themselves to the class, or create a new, multilayered, hypermedia product. Once the teacher uploads the task, he or she can choose to keep the VoiceThread content private, share it, or make it public for all to see. (See figure 6.3.)

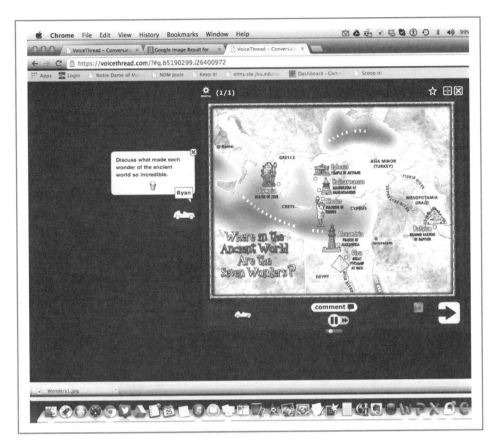

Source: VoiceThread. Used with permission.

Figure 6.3: VoiceThread screenshot.

Tag Clouds

Tag clouds are visual displays summarizing all of the words or topics on a website or field of text. Words or tags that appear most frequently throughout a field of text are displayed in a larger font than words that appear less frequently. Web-based tag cloud generators can quickly build stimulating and colorful word designs. They are considered to be a form of visual art. Following are some of the more popular tag cloud sites.

- Wordle: www.wordle.net

- Tagxedo: www.tagxedo.com

- TagCrowd: http://tagcrowd.com

Students can easily adapt tag clouds into visually appealing mind maps that illustrate an understanding of a given topic. By copying and pasting the text of a reading passage, a tag cloud generator creates a visual summary of the passage for readers by identifying and showcasing the main themes in large, colorful text. To add a fun element to the mundane, students may choose to prepare for the traditional spelling test by creating a tag cloud. Teachers can assess the test by viewing the tag clouds once they are finished. Finally, students are able to record and study specialized or technical vocabulary by creating tag clouds and using the power of the colorful display to promote memorization. (See figure 6.4.)

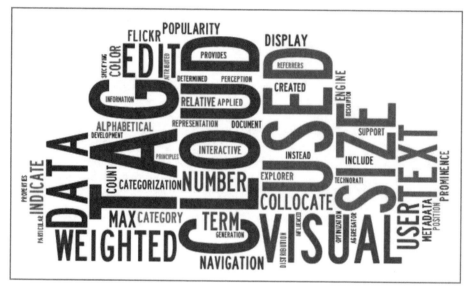

Figure 6.4: A word cloud created with Tagxedo using http://en.wikipedia .org/wiki/Tag_cloud as the text source.

Audio Bytes

Another tool involving multimedia is audio bytes. Teachers and students can take a short video clip and remove or mute the audio. Independently or collaboratively, students can create their own narration based on the clip or content. Depending on the video clip, students can be guided to perform a wide variety of audio byte activities. In science, teachers can mute the video of an animal show and have the students create their own Discovery or National Geographic documentary. In reading, students can perform voice-overs of favorite stories such as *The Three Little Pigs* or *The Twelve Labors of Hercules* that were originally produced as plays or movies. Just about any video with educational content can be stripped of its audio content, allowing students to take an active role in learning the content of the video or writing personalized scripts for narration.

Additional Strategies, Apps, and Resources to Explore

What follows next is a section with even more strategies, apps, and resources to consider using with the always-on generation.

Mind Mapping

Mind mapping is a time-honored brainstorming strategy that takes a visual approach to exploring topics or central research themes. Students collect, organize, and represent ideas, tasks, words, or other items linked to and arranged around a central theme.

Although the pencil-and-paper approach will work (and work well), numerous apps and services are available to add an additional level of connection between the main theme and supporting ideas. Today, Inspiration and Kidspiration are the most popular mind-mapping tools. Both have wonderful features that include embedding hyperlinks, sound, and even movie files. A wide variety of clip art and templates help create a visual mash-up that students can use to demonstrate their understanding of a topic or create a visually appealing product. Teachers can use it to scaffold an assignment or record a class discussion in a graphic organizer. Other similar apps or digital tools include:

- Mindomo—www.mindomo.com
- Coggle—https://coggle.it
- MindMeister—www.mindmeister.com
- Popplet—http://popplet.com
- XMind—www.xmind.net
- Bubbl.us—https://bubbl.us
- Lucidchart—www.lucidchart.com

Prezi: https://prezi.com

Prezi is an easy-to-use cloud-based presentation app with many of the features you would find in Microsoft PowerPoint or Apple's Keynote. Prezi's "zooming canvas" opens up the classroom to visual, active learning and interactivity, making teacher and student presentations understandable, memorable, and fun. Prezi allows users to insert text, images, and videos that provide a unique visual experience. Students can use Prezi to present to their classmates in any subject area or to complete any project requirement. The app also allows multiple users to edit the same presentation anytime, anywhere. It's also an easy online platform that can be used to create and share student portfolios. The best part is that Prezi is free and available online and for both Apple and Android devices.

Animoto: http://animoto.com

Animoto is an online video creation tool that produces theater-quality productions from simple user images and video clips. Using Animoto's patented Cinematic Artificial Intelligence technology, students and teachers can easily generate wonderful multimedia products with copyright-free music. The video is shared by a hyperlink, making it portable as long as the user has an Internet connection. Animoto is free and available online or for Apple and Google devices.

Magnify It

This low-tech but powerful visual strategy helps students focus on a specific area of a displayed image on an overhead, document camera, LCD projector, or interactive whiteboard. As a way of promoting visual discovery, the teacher or student uses a piece of white paper or cardboard to isolate a region of an image. Students can then be guided to examine the highlighted area and answer questions or provide interpretations related to the image's content. Whether visually dissecting aerial photographs, examining primary sources, or exploring the principles of composition and graphical design, Magnify It is an easy, versatile, and engaging strategy for helping students develop visual fluency. (See figure 6.5.)

Source: Teacher's Curriculum Institute. Used with permission.

Figure 6.5: Magnify It in action.

Digital Collage

Creating a digital collage of powerful images is a versatile strategy that can be used in all subject areas. Teachers can utilize this simple visual approach for motivation, guided learning, and personal reflection—all of which are effective catalysts for discovery-based learning. Teachers or students are asked to collect powerful images without captions that represent different aspects of a topic. Students are asked to make connections between the images in the collage, and provide a personal interpretation of the message conveyed. Google Images is a wonderful resource for planning this strategy. While this can be a powerful strategy for developing visual fluency, it's important to be mindful of possible copyright issues. Beyond this, it is important to prescreen all images to ensure that they are of high quality, relevance, and age appropriateness.

Summarizing the Main Points

This section provides readers with a recap of important information covered in the chapter.

- The older generations used images to supplement text, while the digital generations use text to supplement images.

- Adding images to content helps individuals recall information with amazing accuracy over extended periods of time.

- Colors have a powerful psychological impact on people and appeal to the visual learner. Using the right combination of colors together with visuals when developing learning resources can help engage students.

- To the digital generations, images and video are powerful enough on their own to communicate a message.

- Chronic digital bombardment has sharpened the digital generations' visual abilities.

- The undeniable truth is that the digital generations are driving the modern world toward an irreversible shift from written media to visual media.

Questions to Consider

Now that you've finished the chapter, consider the following questions.

1. How do older generations compare with the digital generations with respect to the use of text and images?

2. How does the use of high-quality images improve the retention of information?

3. If the digital generations have such a strong connection to visuals in the classroom, what does this mean for traditional learning approaches?

4. How can students and educators use visual media to develop powerful and compelling learning experiences?

5. What strategies can parents and educators use to help students be more critical viewers of the visual media they encounter?

For up-to-date resource materials
related to this chapter, please visit
http://bit.ly/Attributes_of_Digital_Learners.

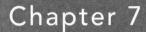

Chapter 7

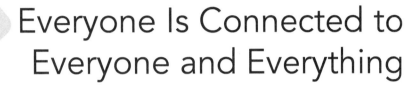

Everyone Is Connected to Everyone and Everything

Individually, we are one drop. Together, we are an ocean.

—Ryunosuke Satoro

Learning Attribute 4

Digital learners prefer to network and collaborate simultaneously with many others. Traditionally, many teachers prefer students to work independently before they network and interact with others in small groups and whole classroom activities.

Stop and take a moment to think about the older generations' world growing up. Consider the limited technologies and means of communication we had available to us. Our world was about movies, records, tape recorders, television, telegrams, radio, telephone, cameras, projectors, VCRs, and filmstrips. When we were students, we were often expected to initially work independently when new information was being introduced. Outside of school, there were really only two ways we were able to immediately communicate with others—in person and by telephone.

Now think about the digital world of today: computers, laptops, tablets, smartphones, Bluetooth, Wi-Fi, video mash-ups, Instagram, Snapchat, Skype, Facebook, texting, tweeting, social networking, and so on. The digital generations have grown up with literally dozens, if not hundreds, of different ways to communicate—an amazing collection of different tools used for different types of communication to different groups.

And since many of these tools have been available to them for their entire lives, the digital generations have completely internalized their use and take these tools for granted. The Internet is a natural space for them. It's fully integrated and commonplace in their world. They now live a hybrid existence—combining physical and virtual worlds into a seamless network of communications, information, entertainment, and sharing. This new existence can be perplexing to some members of the older generations, because it is so different than their experiences growing up.

In her book *It's Complicated: The Social Lives of Networked Teens*, author danah boyd (2014) explains several factors that have led to this dramatic move toward social media by the digital generations. Many adults throw around the term *addiction* to describe the digital generations' apparently constant need to be connected to their online worlds. It is important to emphasize that the digital generations are not addicted to online behavior—or to technology, for that matter. They have a constant need to socialize using whatever outlets are available to them. Consider the location of their friends in comparison to their homes. Oftentimes, the digital generations can't simply walk next door to visit a friend or group of friends.

In a world where danger is seen to be lurking just around the corner, there is an increasing culture of fear. Parents are limiting the freedom of teens due to the belief that something bad might happen without constant adult supervision. Gone are the days of the "be back before dark" mentality. The potential threat of predators, gangs, accidents, bullying, and youthful mischief are highlighted daily on the news, causing parents to increasingly lock down their teens' physical freedoms. This lockdown has also occurred in the common social areas teenagers traditionally used to meet. Places such as malls, convenience stores, playgrounds, and schools often have strictly enforced loitering laws that discourage social gatherings. The digital generations, in need of social interaction, seek socialization by the only means they have at their disposal. While in the safety of their homes or school, they have made up for their perceived lack of freedom by migrating their lives more and more to the new digital landscape.

The digital generations are frequently criticized, derided, misunderstood, misrepresented, and disrespected in the press. They're often accused of being intellectual slackers and antisocial beings who lack even the most fundamental social skills. The authors of this book disagree. From our perspective, for the vast majority of the digital generations, the digital world is far from being an isolating experience. Outside of school, they are immersed in a media-participatory culture built on physical or close relationships that allows them to interact not only with their friends, but also with people who are not geographically close to them. The emergence of collective intelligence, crowdsourcing, smart mobs, the global brain, and group IQ have created an entirely new way of processing massive amounts of information by creating a shared pool of knowledge where the collective whole is greater than the sum of the individual parts. The emergence of global networking has shifted power and knowledge from the individual to the group. With the Internet, everyone has become connected to everyone and everything else, allowing individuals to work together to accomplish things collaboratively.

Not so long ago, this kind of instant communication was entirely the subject of science fiction. Now the digital generations are constantly in contact with one another, as thousands of text messages a month would seem to indicate. In fact, they are highly social. The difference is they're just not social in the way that we think.

Global digital networks are pervasive in our society, so virtual interaction is taken for granted and having an enormous impact on daily life. Kids seeking information or playing games today are just as likely to be interacting with, competing against, or collaborating with people from Europe, South America, Africa, the Middle East, or Asia as they are to be interacting with people from their own country. The emergence of the new digital landscape has quite literally led to the death of distance. There has never been a time where distance has meant less than it does today. This holds tremendous implications for education. The new digital landscape provides both teachers and students with opportunities to go beyond the physical barriers of the traditional brick-and-mortar classroom, allowing both digital and nondigital experiences to come to life and prevent student learning from being limited to self-contained, self-constrained physical environments.

One of the best examples of the power of networking and collaboration is the writing of this book. Ian constantly travels around the world while calling Vancouver his home; Nicky spends half of her time in Canada and the other half in New Zealand; and Ryan writes from the comfort of his home office or faculty office in Maryland. At any given time, the three authors may be on different continents and in different time zones. They practice what they preach: editing their chapters on Google Drive, while they talk and debate with one another on Skype.

Beyond working together, Ian, Nicky, and Ryan have developed a close friendship in spite of the differences in ages and nationalities. In fact, Ian and Ryan have only met face to face twice, while Ryan and Nicky have yet to meet in person. Yet the three of them know each other's families, hobbies, and pets.

In the same manner, students and teachers have the ability to leverage the socialized realm of the new digital landscape for effective communication and collaboration with each other and the outside world. Students studying about civil war can talk directly with others in Syria experiencing it. Kids trying to understand the impact of extreme weather can communicate with students in the storm-ravaged Philippines or

New Jersey. Tackling an environmental issue, students can discuss the consequences of the Fukushima Daiichi nuclear reactor meltdown, or examine the aftereffects of the Gulf oil spill by contacting and interviewing local residents. Students can work in virtual partnerships on projects with students from across town or around the world just as easily as from across the room as they develop the essential skills required to operate in the new learning and working environments of the 21st century.

Strategies and Tools That Work

What follows are some examples of learning strategies and web-based tools that help address digital learners' desire to work collaboratively.

Google Drive: www.google.com/drive/download

Google Drive is a powerful suite of online services available through a free Google account. Having much of the same functionality as Microsoft Office programs, Google Drive migrates common application types such as word processing, spreadsheets, and slide shows online and provides the means to share access to these documents with links and permissions. Students experience real-time collaboration and communication using collective intelligence to perform a shared task.

Both students and teachers can easily fashion online quizzes and exit tickets using Google Forms. In a few minutes, a teacher can generate a survey to capture student performance or attitudinal data. Once students have completed this task, their responses populate a spreadsheet for the teacher to view, download, and perform a data analysis they can use to inform future instructional decisions.

For a powerful, collaborative learning experience, provide small groups with an individual Google Doc and watch as text, images, and other content populates the document. Teachers can easily scroll between each document to monitor the teams' progress. Google also offers Presentation, a slide show generator that allows users to collaboratively make creative multimedia products.

Google Drive regularly adds new features to its products. Some of the latest include Google Drawings for freeform art and graphical work, Lucidchart for developing mind maps and flowcharts, and Movenote to present your documents as video with audio commentary (popular for flipped classroom models). (See figure 7.1.)

Source: Google, Inc.

Figure 7.1: Google Drive interface.

Skype

Skype is a free service that provides video and audio Internet calls around the world. Users simply sign up for a free account and develop a list of contacts to communicate with.

Using a computer, tablet, or smartphone connected to the Internet, teachers and students can arrange Skype conversations with experts or guest speakers; teachers and students can connect with classrooms in other cities, states, provinces, or countries to explore diversity and develop new learning partnerships; and teachers can conduct online meetings, conferences, tutoring sessions, or offer virtual office hours.

Imagine students learning about an impending storm from a meteorologist, poetry from a Pulitzer Prize–winning author, or earth science from an astronaut. Powerful, easy-to-use videoconferencing software such as Skype eliminates the barriers of distance and time, and provides new opportunities for students to seek knowledge from new outlets. (See figure 7.2.)

Source: Courtesy of Skype in the Classroom. Used with permission.

Figure 7.2: Skype in the Classroom screenshot.

Twitter

Twitter is a very popular microblogging service where users send tweets or comments that are limited to 140 characters. How popular is Twitter? It's so popular that it only takes about three minutes for Twitter's one billion users to generate one million tweets. That's more than five hundred million tweets daily (Smith, 2014d).

Students and teachers can use hashtags to moderate a backchannel during classroom discussions. *Backchanneling* is text-based online commentary that takes place in real time simultaneously with live spoken remarks. A *hashtag* is a word or phrase preceded by a hash sign (#), used on social media sites to identify messages about a specific topic. By including a hashtag with a descriptor, users can filter tweets into categories and bring a new dimension to classroom interaction that can continue when class is over. Twitter can also be used as a digital bulletin board, for homework reminders, as an archive for absent students, as an online debate forum, and to gather feedback or data. It is also a great way to connect to other teachers and share ideas, read good content, and participate in academic discourse. (See figure 7.3.)

Source: Twitter.

Figure 7.3: Twitter screenshot.

Padlet

Padlet is an online workspace that displays content created by users in real time. With a freeform or stream display, visitors add posts to the wall. Anyone visiting the wall can see all of the previously submitted content. Teachers, facilitators, and trainers are able to share a link and provide access to individuals so they can brainstorm ideas, work on a collaborative project, curate hyperlinks to resources, take notes, create posters or brochures, plan events, or conduct online discussions. Padlet is great for all grade levels and content areas.

Wikis

Using the same philosophy as Wikipedia, wikis allow multiple editors to cumulatively add and modify subject content on a webpage. Adopted by many school systems, organizations, and higher education institutions, wikis are a great way to collaborate online, share and create content, and manage projects with little to no coding needed. Wiki users are able to add text, images, videos, and documents with relative ease. With hundreds of add-ons and widgets available, wiki collaborators can create newsfeeds and embed content from other web resources such as Poll Everywhere, YouTube, or Google Calendar.

There are numerous wiki services available for free for educators. Each is relatively easy to use and contains useful tutorials and help menus. Wikispaces, PBworks, and Zoho Wiki are examples of free services available to teachers and students.

Additional Strategies, Apps, and Resources to Explore

What follows is a section with more strategies, apps, and resources to consider using with the always-on generation.

TodaysMeet: https://todaysmeet.com

TodaysMeet helps teachers and students embrace the power of backchanneling. Students are able to ask questions or post comments based on a lecture or a general reaction to the class they are attending (or even a class that has ended). After class, teachers can visit the backchannel and answer questions or address comments to provide closure to the lesson. If student groups are presenting, then others can respond to or comment on the content of the presentation without antagonizing or distracting the group during the presentation process. At a later date, presenters can view the comments and adjust presentation content based on the feedback provided.

Remind101: www.remind101.com

Remind101 is a safe way for students and teachers to send and receive text messages without the privacy concerns of sharing mobile phone numbers. Remind101 acts as an intermediary service and safely routes messages from teachers to students and parents. Remind101 uses mobile learning to keep students and parents informed and updated about upcoming projects, special events, or important announcements.

Blogs

Weblogs, or blogs for short, are a digital version of interactive journals organized by entries that are referred to as blog posts. Blogs are extremely popular, because they make sharing ideas, opinions, and viewpoints easy to do without users needing to know advanced coding or web design. In a matter of minutes, anyone with Internet access can create and post comments to a captive and authentic audience. Many blog services offer readers the opportunity to leave comments for authors and other readers, which encourages the free flow of ideas. Google Blogger, WordPress, and Tumblr are among a few of the many free, easy-to-use blogging services available. In fact, the authors of this book collaborate on a blog. Please visit *InfoSavvy 21* (www.infosavvy21.com/blog) to read content related to 21st century education and learning in the digital age. (See figure 7.4.)

Figure 7.4: *InfoSavvy 21* blog screenshot.

In addition, here are four professional education blogs we are big fans of.

- *Edutopia*: www.edutopia.org

- *MindShift*: http://blogs.kqed.org/mindshift

- *TeachThought*: www.teachthought.com

- *Edudemic*: www.edudemic.com

Google Groups

With Google Groups, teachers and students can create online and email-based discussion forums. Online forums allow extended conversations to occur between multiple participants. Teachers could create a group specifically for a class or topic and invite group members to join and participate. During the course of a Google Group's online forum, participants can use computers, laptops, tablets, or smartphones to post messages to one another, upload files for review, or collaborate on a webpage.

Straw Poll: http://strawpoll.me

Straw Poll is a simple method for creating a quick poll with teachers, parents, and students. No sign-up is necessary. You simply visit Straw Poll to create a poll and share a hyperlink with participants so they can respond to it. Poll data are instantly generated and shared once the voting has taken place. Teachers can use Straw Poll to generate an exit poll or ticket that asks students to share their opinion on a topic and generate authentic data to use during a lesson. (See figure 7.5.)

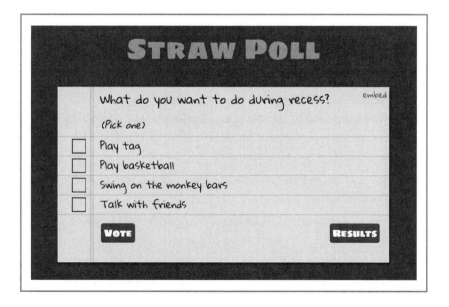

Source: Straw Poll. Used with permission.

Figure 7.5: Straw Poll sample.

Summarizing the Main Points

This section provides readers with a recap of important information from the chapter.

- Digital learners prefer to network and collaborate simultaneously with others.

- The digital generations have grown up with hundreds of different ways to communicate and stay connected.

- The digital generations are not necessarily addicted to their digital devices. In fact, they are highly social beings who use the most convenient and effective methods to constantly stay in contact with their friends and the world.

- The emergence of global networking has shifted power and knowledge from the individual to a collective intelligence. Everybody is potentially connected to everyone and everything else.

- The new digital landscape allows both teachers and students to go beyond the physical classroom and eliminates student learning from being limited to a single environment.

- The strategies, apps, and resources listed in this chapter help promote collaboration and connectedness amongst students.

Questions to Consider

Now that you've finished the chapter, consider the following questions.

1. What implications does the move to the digital landscape have for the future of learning?

2. How has the emergence of new digital technologies changed the way that you and your students communicate in and out of the classroom?

3. How has collective intelligence changed the need for rote memorization in schools and life?

4. How has knowledge distribution changed from the pre-Internet days to today, with the emergence of the new digital landscape?

5. Why are the members of the digital generations so comfortable moving between the real world and the digital landscape?

For up-to-date resource materials related to this chapter, please visit http://bit.ly/Attributes_of_Digital_Learners.

Chapter 8

Fast Pattern Reading

*Education has produced a vast population able to read
but unable to distinguish what is worth reading.*

—G. M. TREVELYAN

Learning Attribute 5

Digital readers unconsciously read text on a page or on a screen in an *F* or
fast pattern. Most adults in the western world have been conditioned to
unconsciously read text in a *Z* pattern. Today's digital generations read in a
pattern that's very different from the way we learned in school.

First, some background: Images have the ability to quickly portray meaning. It only takes 150 milliseconds for the brain to process images and 100 milliseconds more to attach meaning to the images. The eye processes the content of photographs 60,000 times faster than the eye processes and interprets the content of text and words (Burmark, 2002). That's why infographics are so popular—they're engaging, colorful, and easy to digest, such as figure 8.1 (page 84).

As they scan and read the infographic, readers are drawn into a visual narrative; using predominantly images supported by text, digital readers quickly capture and interpret vast amounts of information (Estes, 2014).

Seventy percent of our body's sensory receptors are in our eyes, and 30 percent of the nerve cells in the brain's cortex are devoted to visual processing (compared to only about 8 percent for touch and about 3 percent for hearing). It turns out we're all, at our very core, inherently visual learners. So it's completely natural that today's students might be far more inclined toward visual processing and text processing because their brains are designed that way (Antranik, 2011).

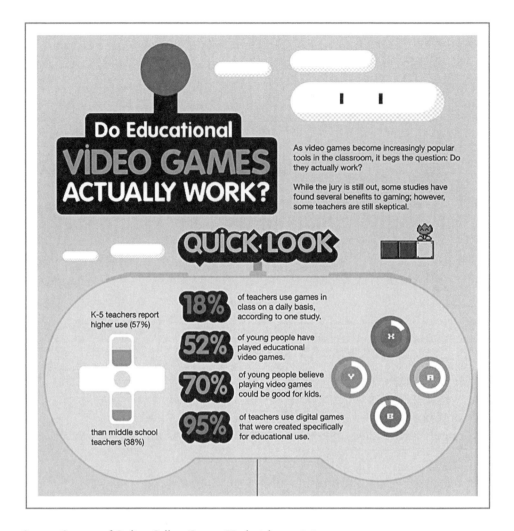

Source: Courtesy of Online College Course. Used with permission.

Figure 8.1: Example of an infographic.

Eighty percent of our information comes through our eyes. Our eyes have the resolution of a 576-megapixel camera, while most high-end digital cameras claim to have a resolution of 24 megapixels. Every second, our eyes take in 72 gigabytes of information. In fact, our eyes are the world's greatest cameras. They use 86 billion neurons to interpret visual data and bring it to life (Cartier-Wells, 2013). As a result, the brain is much more designed for processing visual information than anything else, so it's completely understandable that today's students might be far more inclined toward visual processing than text processing.

Recently, it was discovered that because of chronic digital bombardment, digital readers' eyes move in a very different way than traditional readers' eyes move when it comes to scanning a page, reading materials, and searching for information. The eyes of traditional readers unconsciously find an intersection approximately one-third of the way down the page, and one-third of the page in from the side. The Greeks called this intersection the golden mean. When traditional readers start reading for information, their eyes read in what is called a *Z* curve or *Z* pattern.

They use a simple *Z* curve if there's only a small amount of information on a page. (See figure 8.2.)

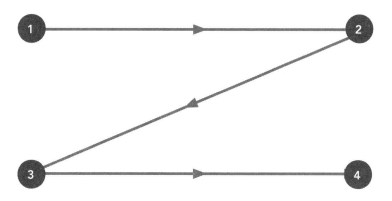

Source: Used with permission from Steve Bradley.

Figure 8.2: Example of simple Z pattern.

And they use a complex *Z* curve or zigzag pattern that involves a series of *Z* movements if there's lots of information on the page (figure 8.3).

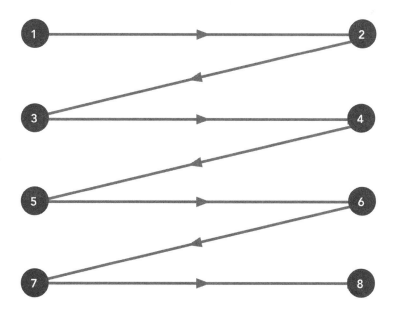

Source: Used with permission from Steve Bradley.

Figure 8.3: Example of zigzag pattern.

The zigzag pattern is how many of the older generations read large blocks of text. However, new research has demonstrated that digital readers don't read a page the way that older generations do. Instead, their eyes first unconsciously skim the bottom of the page and then scan the edges of the page, before they start scanning the page itself for information in what's called an *F* or fast pattern. *F* pattern reading has three components:

1. Users read in a horizontal movement, usually across the upper part of the content area. This initial element forms the F's top bar.

2. Next, users move down the page a bit and read across in a second horizontal movement that typically covers a shorter area than the previous movement. This additional element forms the F's lower bar.

3. Finally, users scan the content's left side in a vertical movement. Sometimes this is a fairly slow and systematic scan that appears as a solid stripe on an eye-tracking heat map. Other times, users move faster, creating a spottier heat map. This last element forms the F's stem (figure 8.4).

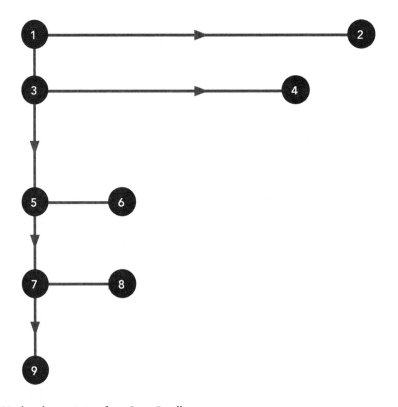

Source: Used with permission from Steve Bradley.

Figure 8.4: Example of *F* pattern.

Although the *F* is not always perfectly shaped in the scans (sometimes the scans can resemble the capital letter *E* or *L*), the general shape roughly resembles a capital letter *F* (Nielsen, 2006). What you see in figure 8.5 is a series of images captured at Kent State University. Researchers there used heat maps to track the eye movements of readers in different reading configurations, and then summarized the results. When looking at and interpreting these maps, what you need to appreciate is that the brighter the color, the more the readers have focused on the information in that area of the page. And, conversely, the darker the area, the less the readers have focused on that area of the page. Digital readers unconsciously ignore the right side and the bottom half of the page. It turns out that they will only go to the right side or the bottom of the page if and only if they are highly motivated to do so. At most, they will only read about 28 percent of the words on a page—an average of 20 percent is more likely. In fact, you can literally draw a diagonal line from the upper right-hand corner of a page to the lower left-hand corner of a page, and typically, unless you find a way to attract and engage digital readers, they just won't go below that line.

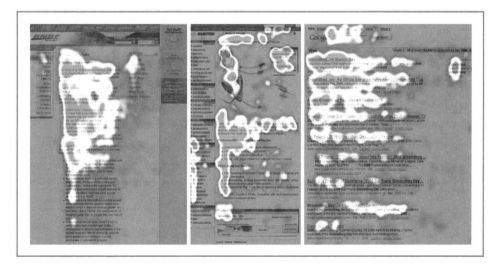

Figure 8.5: *F* pattern thermographic heat scans.

The initial conclusion seems to be that the *F* pattern mimics the way digital readers play video games and surf the web scanning the screen for information.

Strategies and Tools That Work

This section is slightly different in this chapter than in the previous ones. It describes some best practices for both teachers and students as they design paper-based or digital materials. The following strategies are helpful tips to making visual materials that are impactful for the intended audiences.

Implications of the *F* Pattern

The *F* pattern's implications for reading are clear. Readers won't read text thoroughly in a word-by-word manner. Exhaustive reading is rare, so the most important information should be placed across the top of the page in the first two paragraphs where it will generally be read. Lesser information should be placed along the left edge of the design in bullet points where little horizontal eye movement is required to take everything in. Start subheads, paragraphs, and bullet points with impactful information-carrying words that users will notice when scanning down the left side of content in the final part of the stem of the *F* pattern. They'll read the third word on a line much less often than the first two words.

The Power of the Eye

A study of cereal aisles at grocery stores found cereal products marketed to kids are placed half as high on shelves as cereals marketed for adults, so they can appear closer to eye level. The characters on the kids' cereal boxes, such as the Trix Rabbit and Cap'n Crunch, also appear to be looking downwards at a 9.7-degree angle, whereas characters on adult boxes look straight ahead. The researchers said this marketing strategy of having cartoon characters lock eyes with children may influence their connection with a brand, fostering loyalty and inspiring their interest in the products (Jaslow, 2014).

Our eyes are the gateway to the mind. Effective materials are designed to stimulate the eyes so they're naturally drawn to the visual component of materials. Pictorial information increases the speed and retention of your message. Pictures represent information and communicate ideas in completely different ways than words and convey emotions and facts simultaneously. The effect of an image is instantaneous, and viewers respond without conscious thought. Images have now become an integral part of our communications; this has made visual literacy a critical element in today's visual world.

> Visual content is huge online right now. It's increased 9,900 percent on the Internet since 2007, and for good reason. Visual data provides us with relief from today's era of information overload. We receive five times more information today than we did in 1986—about 100,500 words outside of work every day. People get exhausted from consuming plain black text on a white background all the time. It makes sense that we crave color and design, because

we're programmed to. Almost half of your brain is involved in visual processing, and that half is pretty good at what it does. You can make sense of a visual in less than 1/10 of a second. Instead of hoping that your viewers choose your content as part of their 100,500 daily word count, create a chart or graphic that appeals to their visual wiring. (Jones, 2014)

Humans process images much faster than they process text; similarly, photographs are processed much faster than clip art. Whenever possible, use photos rather than clip art, as the eye instantly discerns the difference. Generally, the rule is to have only one dominant image on a page. It should be an image that clearly complements the content of the page.

Only add images that reinforce or extend your message. It's tempting to add images just for the sake of adding images, but images must be relevant to the message being conveyed. There is nothing more distracting to the reader than an image that has no context to the content of the page or one from a different time period than the content.

Although this is not a hard-and-fast rule, generally try to position images on the right side of the page, leaving lots of white space around the image. Also adhere to the rule of thirds and place the image at one of the two right-side intersections: one-third of the way down the page and one-third of the page in from the right hand side of the page, or two-thirds of the way down the page and two-thirds in from the right hand side of the page.

Things to Remember When Using Images

There are several key elements both teachers and students should consider when using images during the learning process.

Proportion

Try to place only one image on a page. There is no formula for determining the size of an image, but the image shouldn't overpower the message contained on the page. Generally, any text should occupy the left half of the page, and the image should occupy the right half of the page.

Relevancy

Images can distract, match, or extend the meaning of the message. "A picture is worth a thousand words" is only true *if* the picture is clearly related to the topic!

Tone, Style, and Theme

Images convey powerful metaphors inside messages and are intended to complement the message. Do the images in your materials have a consistent look and feel throughout? Does the look and feel of the image align with the look and feel of the content?

Charts and Graphs

Charts and graphs are excellent for communicating significant numbers and statistics to a reader. Charts need titles, clear labeling, and legends. Pie charts work well to show parts or percentages of a whole. However, it's best not to use any more than eight slices in a pie chart. You can highlight a particular slice by making it darker or a brighter color than the others. Bar charts with more than eight elements should be made vertical or down in order to increase readability. About chart colors: In all graph types, cool colors tend to recede information while warm colors bring the information forward. It's best to use primary colors for high contrast, which allows them to be easily distinguished from one another. Avoid putting similar colors together, for example, white and yellow, or dark blue and dark brown. If a color chart is to be printed for black-and-white handouts, ensure that the bars and pie wedges can be easily distinguished by different shades of gray.

Technical Quality

Visual images need to be high quality to be effective. Bitmap digital images, for example, are made up of a grid of dots or pixels of different colors. When a small bitmap image is stretched larger, a pixelated effect is created, with each pixel becoming a larger block of pixels. The result is a coarse and bumpy image of poor quality that becomes a distraction to the reader. (See figure 8.6 for an example.)

Figure 8.6: Example of a pixelated versus a nonpixelated image.

Apparent Motion

Have you ever walked downtown in a big city and spotted someone looking upward? What did you do? Looked up, of course! This is the power of apparent motion. When designing reading materials, you can use the principles of apparent motion to direct an individual's attention to a specific place on the page by using images that depict someone or something in motion.

Apparent motion can be represented by the direction and speed implied by an image. An image of a person walking, riding a bike, skiing, or even looking or pointing in a direction unconsciously forces the viewer's eyes in the direction of the apparent motion.

Although they're no longer around, a good example of this is the old cigarette ads, which were required to print a large warning at the bottom that told you that using this product could kill you. To counter this requirement, ad agencies put an image of someone pointing or moving away from the warning right above the message. Because of apparent motion, most readers never saw the warning! Thus, just as using apparent motion forces you to look away from the warning, it can be used to draw a viewer's focus to a specific part of a page.

Pictures of people and animals need to be placed on a page with care. Generally people and animals need to face inward or toward the message area, *not* outward. Use apparent motion to direct a reader's eyes to focus on *main points* or key ideas on a page. If images are improperly placed, readers' eyes will follow the apparent motion right off the page, and you will lose them.

The Impact of Color on the Audience

According to 3M research (Vogel, Dickson, & Lehman, 1986), the use of color in your materials:

- Increases willingness to read by up to 80 percent
- Increases motivation and participation by up to 80 percent
- Enhances learning and improves retention by more than 75 percent
- Accounts for 60 percent of the acceptance or rejection of an idea
- Outsells black-and-white advertising by 88 percent

Typefaces or Fonts

A typeface is a collection of characters, letters, and symbols that have a unique design. For example, Garamond, Times New Roman, and Arial are typefaces. Typefaces must align with your message and make words easy to read by providing a suitable tone and background. If a typeface calls undue attention to itself or is difficult to read, it becomes a distraction to the reader.

Number of Typefaces

Any number of typefaces and styles are readily available for users of all ages. Novice users often select many typefaces for the same page or document, which can create a "ransom note" effect. A general guideline is to use no more than two fonts from the same typeface family on the same page.

Typeface Moods

Because they have a body language, typefaces express different moods to different people. These moods can be academic, bossy, soothing, old, happy, humorous, formal, contemporary, futuristic, and so on. It is important to try to identify typefaces that align with the mood and perspectives of your audience, as well as being aligned to the theme, tone, or mood of the page or document.

Serif Fonts

These typefaces have tiny horizontal or vertical lines added at the ends of longer line strokes. Serif fonts are highly readable. They unconsciously facilitate the ease of eye movement across each line of text, making them very useful for large paragraphs of text as well as headlines, ads, and letterheads.

Sans Serif Fonts

These fonts don't use serifs or little lines at the ends of the line strokes. They are simple strokes of equal weight or thickness with a clean and smooth look. Sans serif fonts are highly noticeable. They get a reader's attention quickly and easily, but the lack of serifs tends to slow down the reader's eye. Sans serif fonts should be saved for headlines or titles, and not large blocks of text. (See figure 8.7 for examples of serif and sans serif fonts.)

> # This example uses a serif font.

> # This example uses a sans serif font.

Figure 8.7: Example of serif versus sans serif fonts.

Capital Letters

Limit use of capital letters. When we read, our eyes capture the shapes of whole words, including the extensions of letters above and below the normal letter size. However, when text is WRITTEN IN ALL CAPITALS, no ascenders or descenders are used. Because words using all capital letters have nearly the same visual shape, this slows down the reader. All capital words are significantly less readable than sentences that use upper- and lowercase letters.

Font Color

Clarity of communication can be enhanced by making a strong contrast between the color of the text and the color of the background. For example, using light text on a dark background or dark text on a light background enhances the readability of the text.

Font Weight

Typefaces that are too dark can blur the text. Typefaces that are too light make it hard to read. It's better to err on the side of light fonts because they appear simpler and cleaner. If you must, use shadows for titles, but not for the body text.

Underlining, Bold, and Italics

Underlining is passé today. Use *italics* for emphasis within text. Use *italics* sparingly but not for extended blocks of text, because it bores or tires the eye. **Bold** is good for headlines as it makes words jump out and grabs the audience's attention, but is too strong for body text. *Italics* whisper, while **bold** shouts.

Justification and Readability

The alignment of type between margins is called text justification. There are four possibilities: left, right, full, and center justification.

Generally, text that is left justified is more readable and less formal than fully justified text. This is because in the western world, we tend to read from left to right, and our eyes look for an indicator that the line being read is coming to an end. Full justification makes this much harder for the eye to determine.

Summarizing the Main Points

This section provides readers with a recap of important information covered in the chapter.

- Traditional readers tend to read in a *Z* or zigzag pattern.

- Digital readers unconsciously read text on a page or on a screen in an *F* or fast pattern.

- Humans process images much faster than they process text; similarly, photographs are processed much faster than clip art.

- Effective materials should be designed to stimulate the eyes. The eyes are naturally drawn to the visual components of materials.

- Use apparent motion to direct a reader's eyes to focus on main points or key ideas on a page.

Questions to Consider

Now that you've finished the chapter, consider the following questions.

1. What is the difference between *F* pattern and *Z* pattern reading?

2. What implications does *F* pattern reading hold for teaching, learning, and assessment?

3. How can an understanding of *F* pattern reading help in the design of engaging reading materials that will compel readers to read the entire page for information?

4. What is apparent motion, and how can it be used to focus readers' attention?

5. What are some of the principles of graphic design that should be considered in the design of learning materials?

For up-to-date resource materials
related to this chapter, please visit
http://bit.ly/Attributes_of_Digital_Learners.

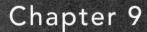

Chapter 9

Just-in-Case Versus Just-in-Time Learning

Change is not merely necessary to life—it is life.

—ALVIN TOFFLER

Learning Attribute 6

Digital learners prefer "just in time" learning. Many educators teach "just in case" learning.

Let's start by asking a question: How many of you had a parent who worked at the same job, or worked in the same industry, for more than twenty years? Many, we suspect. Those were different times. In the past, it was common for people to spend their entire working lifetime in a single career. For example, Ian's dad worked for the same company for thirty-five years. Today, the idea of having a single career for life is very uncommon. We live in a *Hunger Games* economy, where it's everyone for his- or herself, circumstances are constantly changing, and fundamental uncertainty and instability are the new normal.

For the longest time, we've heard estimates that students today should anticipate having four to seven careers in their lifetime. In their critically acclaimed book *The New Division of Labor: How Computers Are Creating the Next Job Market*, writers Frank Levy and Richard Murnane (2004) state that today's generations of students should not anticipate having four to seven careers—they should anticipate having ten to seventeen or more careers (not *jobs* working in the same industry, but *distinct careers*) by the time they're thirty-eight years old.

To be clear, having ten to seventeen or more careers should not be interpreted as a sign of failure or lack of commitment or self-discipline on the part of modern workers. What it reflects is the new economy, and the new employment reality work-ers are facing today where the average length of stay in any job will only be about eighteen to thirty-six months (Meister, 2012).

Today, we live in a time of increasingly disposable information. Often knowledge and skills acquired by the age of twenty are obsolete by the age of forty, if not before. As a result, it is easy to project that today's students will have to replace almost their entire body of knowledge several times during their working lives. Increasingly, we're living in a world where people have to manage their careers and constantly figure out what their next move is to keep themselves relevant and employed in an ever-changing economy!

Right before our very eyes, everything has shifted. In place of the old school-to-work model, we now live in a new age that can best be described as school-to-work-to-school-to-work, repeat. If there's one certainty about what today's digital gener-ations will be doing a decade or two from now, it's that they won't all be doing the same thing, and they certainly won't be drawing on the same body of knowledge that people are using today.

The global economy has created a new division of labor that rewards people who can make swift, well-informed decisions utilizing multiple information sources. At the same time, it penalizes those who lack the new basic skills needed for the new workforce. As a result, our students enter a working world where people need contin-uous upgrading of their skills to stay abreast of, let alone move ahead in, careers. In this new working environment, lifelong learning is mandatory because it is the only insurance against being blindsided by the short shelf life of information.

Even more controversially, Levy and Murnane (2004) suggest that the skills stu-dents need to be successful in college are a different set of skills, not to mention a lesser set of skills, than those needed to be successful in life and work. As a result, students today don't just need a four-year degree—in fact, a university degree is probably only one of many options—and having a degree is probably not enough. What students will really need is to prepare for forty years of ongoing learning and unlearning and relearning.

Beyond this, because of the rapidly changing nature of the economy, it's easy to project that the top ten in-demand jobs that will be available ten years from now probably don't exist today. In the new economy, we are literally preparing students for jobs that don't exist, using technologies that haven't been invented, to solve prob-lems we haven't even begun to anticipate. So as educators, one of the questions we need to be regularly asking ourselves is this: "If our students are competing not just locally, regionally, and nationally, but also globally, with both people and increasingly machines, for jobs and careers that don't yet exist, how do we create learning experiences for a world and a new economy that also don't yet exist?"

Many observers are completely oblivious to just how interconnected all the economies and the people of the world are. So unless we can also change our assumptions about teaching and learning and assessment of that learning, we can't really expect to get anything different from what we're already getting. Meaningful and effective change requires students to have a fundamentally different set of skills than those required to fill in a bubble test or complete a written exam.

The problem is that education today is primarily organized around the just-in-case (JiCTL) model of teaching and learning. The message sent to students is that you have to learn this information just in case it happens to be on the exam, just in case you might need to know it in order to pass the course, just in case you require it to graduate, and just in case you eventually might want to become an engineer or a writer or a doctor.

There absolutely is a place for JiCTL. But because of their digital mindsets, digital learners prefer to learn things not only just in case, but also just in time. They are the "on demand" generation. They are not used to waiting for anything because in the new digital landscape, anything they want to know is just a click away. Their mindset is "Why do I need to memorize huge amounts of information when I can just google it or ask Siri?"

The digital generations have both the desire and the ability to acquire the necessary skills and knowledge just in time to solve a problem, just in time to play a new video game, just in time to play their new favorite song on the piano, just in time to coordinate a gathering, just in time to settle an argument, or just in time to do something they don't yet know how to do, using YouTube, Twitter, Snapchat, Facebook, texting, or hundreds of other readily available online tools.

Just-in-time teaching and learning (JiTTL) offers a blended instructional approach that uses feedback between classroom activities and work that students do at home in preparation for future classroom activities. JiTTL moves away from teacher-centered instruction to a model of discovery learning that provides real-world, personally relevant, highly motivating challenges to students as the main vehicle for progressively introducing activities and new concepts.

The JiTTL model is interactive and engaging for both students and teachers. Like teachers, students must prepare in advance for upcoming learning experiences. To prime and motivate students, teachers present them with mini-scenarios that include just enough information to pique their interest. The scenario contains an essential question—a question that is broad and open-ended, and requires higher-order thinking that can't be easily answered using Google, Yahoo, or Bing.

The final piece of the scenario involves presenting students with a real-world challenge or a simulation of a real-world problem. For example, imagine teaching a geography lesson about the features of the Earth's surface, how those features are arranged, and the patterns and processes that create them. Instead of using the traditional stand-and-deliver model, the topic could be introduced using a real-world scenario such as the following:

> In March 2011, an earthquake of 8.9 magnitude triggered a massive tsunami off the east coast of Japan. Like an overflowing bathtub, the ocean rose higher than the land. As a result, entire communities were destroyed. Twenty thousand people lost their lives that day—but that's only part of the tragedy. More than ninety thousand people were left homeless. Today, many of these same people are still without homes. But we don't hear about the ongoing tragedy in Japan, because it's not in the news anymore. There's only sporadic mention of a damaged nuclear reactor that's still spewing radioactivity into the ocean and the atmosphere. And it's not just natural disasters that are happening in Japan.

> We also don't hear about the repeated earthquakes in Christchurch, New Zealand, or the cyclone in the Philippines, or the superstorm in New Jersey, or the floods in Bangladesh—and so we forget. But what if we didn't forget? Maybe we could even do something about it. Maybe we could contribute to the recovery in a meaningful way. Using your knowledge of earthquakes, how could you help people in need somewhere in the world? Come prepared to share your knowledge of earthquakes with the class.

The beauty of the JiTTL model is that it doesn't require a wholesale change in a teacher's instructional paradigm. Teachers can make a shift as their comfort level increases and as they move away from the traditional model of direct instruction, passive learning, and content-based assessment. JiTTL tasks require students independently or collaboratively to examine their present knowledge, add to it, and then apply their newly constructed knowledge to solve real-world problems. The goal of the JiTTL model is for students to assume more personal responsibility for the learning process.

In comparing just-in-case teaching and learning with just-in-time teaching and learning, the fundamental questions we need to ask are: What world are we preparing our students for? Are we preparing them for the just-in-case world of yesterday—just in case they need to pass the test, pass the course, pass the grade, or to graduate? Or, are we helping prepare them for the ten to seventeen or more careers they will have in their working lifetime? Are we preparing them for their future or our past? Are we preparing them for the economy of yesterday and today, or are we preparing them for the world that awaits them once they leave school?"

Strategies and Tools That Work

What follows is a section with more strategies, apps, and resources to consider using with the always-on generation.

YouTube: www.youtube.com

More than three billion videos are viewed on YouTube every day (Smith, 2014b). YouTube has close to a billion unique visitors every month (YouTube, n.d.). What are the lessons we can learn from YouTube's success, and how can we apply them in our classrooms?

We know that today's generations prefer learning using their digital devices. YouTube (which is owned by Google) has taken advantage of this and assembled massive amounts of engaging video-based material in one place. Learners are able to search for a particular topic and find a vast selection of relevant YouTube clips. While watching a video may at first glance seem to be a passive activity, it is in keeping with the JiTTL model. When video clips are selected wisely, there is more than enough information to capture student interest in a topic.

For even more active participation, YouTube has an annotation feature that allows students to respond to what they have seen and make comments. This allows the teacher to review student responses and make changes to the upcoming lessons accordingly.

Students can also create and upload their own YouTube videos as a means of demonstrating a solution to a problem, or their understanding of a concept they have been introduced to. Fellow students can then provide peer feedback to these videos with their comments.

Snapchat

Snapchat is a photo- and video-sharing app with a twist. Sent media disappear seconds after the images or video have been viewed—the sender gets to decide how long a visual will "live" (from one to ten seconds) after it is viewed. Users love Snapchat's spontaneity. It is ideal for use with both staff and students as a means to communicate personal perspectives within a brief time constraint. For example, what would students say to a high-profile political leader, famous entertainer, or historical figure if they had only a minute or less to do so? Similar to other social networking tools, Snapchat is another online realm the always-on generation uses to broadcast their ideas and opinions to others. It is also a tool that their parents have not followed them onto yet like Facebook or Instagram.

Snapchat is no different from the way we interact in face-to-face situations—it's visual chatting in the moment. Our body language, tone, comments, and facial expressions are captured and shared just in time with our friends. The difference is that we can now share perspectives with others around the globe as well as people in the same room.

Flipped Learning

The Khan Academy is known for its flipped classroom model. (See figure 9.1.) The flipped classroom allows students to learn new content by watching videos of teacher lectures and other presentation materials online at home or school before concepts are explored in greater depth in the classroom. While some hail the flipped classroom as being innovative, others believe that this model just maintains the same traditional stand-and-deliver relationship between teachers and students, only now we use technology. What we advocate is flipping the learning. When done well, flipping the learning is a powerful tool for just-in-time learning.

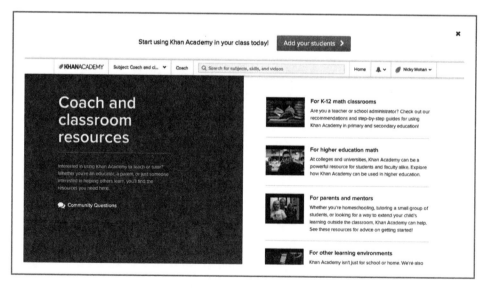

Source: Khan Academy, n.d. Note: All Khan Academy content is available for free at www.khanacademy.org.

Figure 9.1: Khan Academy screenshot.

When used in conjunction with the JiTTL model, students don't just watch a video at home or school as they would passively listen to a lecture in the classroom. Rather, students are actively engaged in the learning process. When using the JiTTL model, students watch the videos to learn more about a particular topic or concept just in time for completing a task or solving a real-world problem. The video is only one of many resources made available for students to gather information.

However, the process is not just intended to help students learn content. It's also about equipping students with the essential skills needed to effectively identify and utilize the most relevant sources. Students gain background knowledge, which prepares them for upcoming activities both in and out of the classroom where they will use the time that would otherwise have been spent on content delivery to engage in higher-order thinking and the application of that thinking.

For example, before a science class, students might be asked to view a video of an experiment that demonstrates the effectiveness of different types of salt in deicing agents. Once viewed, the questions that could be asked might include:

- With the knowledge you have gained from viewing the video, what do you think happened, and what did you notice when different salts were used?

- Which type of salt do you think is most cost-effective, and why do you think that?

- Which type of salt do you think is the safest for the environment, and why do you think that?

- Which type of salt do you think is the best at preventing ice formation, and under what conditions?

In the JiTTL model, videos are used to prompt interest, motivate, and augment student knowledge, which allows for more face-to-face time where teachers and students can work together for deeper learning and which creates more opportunities to apply knowledge and skills to challenging in-class assignments.

Today's students are very visual—they want everything video-based and time-shifted. The best advice is to simply start recording. Don't wait until you have state-of-the-art technology and perfect lighting—it's not broadcasting. The goal and opportunity is to capture and transfer knowledge as it takes place—immediacy of knowledge is invaluable. When combined with JiTTL, flipped learning promotes anytime, anyplace, and any-pace learning opportunities.

Wikis

Wikis are an online tool that allows users to create, add, modify, and delete content in collaboration with others. They are a great tool for enabling the on-demand generation to take control of and shape their own learning, which they do by constructing their own knowledge, making them producers rather than just consumers of content. Working collaboratively and collectively to construct and manage their own knowledge gives students ownership and responsibility for what they learn. Building wikis is an inexpensive and enjoyable way to engage students in all stages of the learning process. Following are the top wiki tools for the classroom.

- Wikispaces.com: Wikispaces is a social writing platform that also acts as a classroom management tool for keeping teachers and students organized and on task. Teachers can use Wikispaces to create assignments and share resources. Not only does the site provide easy-to-use templates, but it's also free and includes a variety of assessment tools.

- Wikidot.com: This site is free and has easy-to-use templates with unlimited page storage, free web hosting, and domain name services.

- PBworks.com: This wiki-like website offers educators a range of options that encourage student-centered learning. Students build websites or webpages that can be shared with other students.

Wikis really complement the JiTTL approach because they encourage collaboration. Teachers can assign projects that require students to continuously communicate to solve real-world problems. Because wikis are customized to what students are learning, wikis can serve as personal "digital textbooks."

For example, in the Common Core State Standards curriculum, there is this Math standard for grade 6: *Solve real-world and mathematical problems involving area, surface area, and volume* (6.6.G.A). Using this standard, students can be set to task with a real-world challenge. They are asked to construct a wiki that will be used to gather, organize, and share the information needed to solve the following problem:

> Your graphic design firm has a new client. It's a local cafe that makes an amazing granola that it wants to start packaging and marketing. Your client has asked you to create mockups of the package in two different shapes of cereal boxes that each holds the same amount of cereal. The client would also like you to come up with a name for the product and design the outside of the package to profile and promote the features of the granola, as well as to develop a promotional campaign for marketing the granola.

For a science or geography unit, students could be asked to construct a wiki to capture and organize important information as they work together as part of a research team investigating global warming or the effect of an oil spill on Hawaii, the Great Barrier Reef, or the Galapagos Islands.

Skype in the Classroom

Skype is a free communication software tool that both teachers and students can use to video chat with one or multiple people at the same time. Skype also allows for audio and text communication, and can be used simultaneously on various electronic devices such as computers, smartphones, and tablets—anything with an Internet connection. Teachers can connect with colleagues, while students can use it to link with other classrooms and experts from around the world.

Field trips are not just expensive; they also require a tremendous amount of planning, which in turn involves time—time that educators never seem to have enough of. Using Skype, experts can come right into your classroom to work directly with your students, have a conversation, and answer questions in real time. Teachers can use videoconferencing to bring authors, content experts, producers, artists, performers, other teachers, and even students right into the classroom to talk directly with their students.

A "mystery Skype" is another way to increase student suspense and engagement. To facilitate this strategy, simply prearrange a conversation with a caller or classroom from another city, state, province, or country. Help students brainstorm questions and establish jobs or roles that each student will have during the mystery Skype. During the conversation, the teacher guides the students through the call, only intervening when absolutely necessary, as students try to determine where the caller or classroom is located. For more detail, please visit http://pernillesripp .com/2011/10/25/so-you-want-to-do-mystery-skype (Ripp, 2011) to learn about this exciting experience.

When used in conjunction with the JiTTL model, students are encouraged to ask teachers questions using a text message option. In this way, students get immediate responses or feedback just in time to complete an assignment, project, or challenge or to get clarification for any questions they may have. Skype also allows students to remotely submit assignments for immediate feedback, and it keeps a record of all conversations and transmitted files, which serves as a tracker for teachers.

Skype can be also be used to deliver bite-size chunks of information to students or groups of students unable to attend class because of illness, weather, or travel, allowing them to collaborate on projects with their teams from their homes or wherever they are at that moment. While Skype by itself promotes student engagement, assigning students roles as recorders, bloggers, mappers, or any other tasks ensures they are not just passively sitting and watching, but actively engaged in the learning process.

Additional Strategies, Apps, and Resources to Explore

The following apps, instructional strategies, and resources are ideal for the JiTTL model. They help students learn "just in time" when it has become imperative for them to do so through circumstance or self-interest.

TED Talks

TED Talks (Technology Entertainment Design) are a set of global conferences whose presentations are captured on video and offered for free viewing online at www.ted.com. To date, more than 1,700 talks have been uploaded. These videos have been viewed more than one billion times worldwide (Phys.org, 2014).

TED Talks are not only enjoyable and informative, but when carefully selected, they can be an effective way of getting students interested in various topics. To complement the JiTTL model, teachers can direct students to post their thoughts on a class wiki or blog or send a Skype message to the teacher. Another exciting possibility is to have students write and deliver their own TED Talk to the class and share it on YouTube. Viewers can offer their opinions on the delivery of the talk, providing constructive feedback.

The Fast Five

If you want students to develop information fluency at the same time they're developing just-in-time skills, have your students do the "fast five." At the beginning of the class, give them five minutes with their digital devices to identify five online resources that will help them learn how to do something new and interesting—write a haiku, tie a tie, make a new food dish, learn to juggle balls, play chess, chart family history, become a Wikipedia editor, create a podcast, sketch an object . . . the list of possibilities is endless.

iTunes U: www.apple.com/education/ipad/itunes-u

iTunes U is a free app available for both the iPad and iPhone that allows teachers to create their own online courses. When teaching using iTunes U courses, everything from assignments and materials to students' study notes is available in one place. Students can see all of the assignments for courses they are enrolled in by date, and check them off as they are completed. All course materials are accessible online, so learning and studying can happen anytime, anywhere, and at any pace using almost any digital device.

New posts can be added to courses at any time, so teachers can update their lessons with current events. iTunes U provides automatic notifications of updates to students' devices, so they'll be prepared for the next class.

Google Hangouts: www.google.com/+/learnmore/hangouts

Google Hangouts is a great social media tool to connect with colleagues, other classrooms, and experts in the field. If taking your students to a museum or heritage site in another country is not possible, try organizing a Google Hangout. This tool allows you to video chat with anyone with an Internet connection. There is even the option to have multiple video calls happen at the same time, so that a group of people can hang out together. Google Hangouts are great for holding discussions or forming a panel that students can address with questions they've written about a topic. (See figure 9.2.)

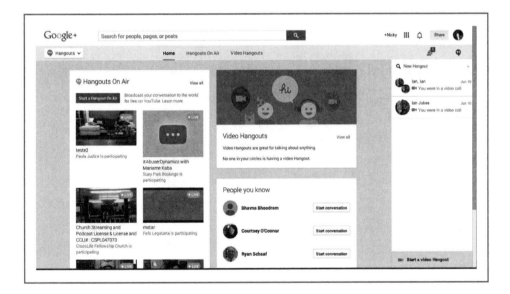

Source: Google, Inc.

Figure 9.2: Google Hangouts screenshot.

Facebook: www.facebook.com

Facebook is a popular, free social networking service available in thirty-seven different languages that connects over one billion registered users ages thirteen years and older. It allows them to create profiles, upload photos and video, send messages, and keep in touch with friends, family, and colleagues. Some Facebook features can be adapted for teacher and student use in the classroom. These include:

- Groups—Allow members with common interests to find each other and interact

- Events—Allow members to publicize an event, invite guests, and track who plans to attend

- Pages—Allow members to create and promote a public page built around a specific topic

Facebook can be used in any number of ways. Teachers can use Facebook to host online discussions or create content on shared pages. Students have an online place where they can ask questions, not only of the teacher, but of each other and experts. Classmates can help each other with tips and suggestions on homework, assignments, projects, and technology. As with any social networking service, much of it is public, so caution is encouraged in regard to privacy issues. (See figure 9.3.)

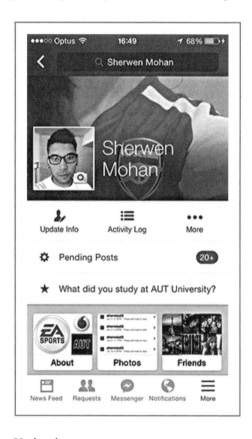

Source: Sherwen Mohan. Used with permission.

Figure 9.3: Facebook screenshot.

Instagram: www.instagram.com

Instagram is an online mobile photo-sharing, video-sharing, and social networking service that enables its users to take pictures and videos, apply digital filters to them, and share them on a variety of social networking services, such as Facebook, Twitter, Tumblr, and Flickr.

As we have indicated in this book, the digital generations are visual learners. Instagram allows teachers to use pictures and video to share classroom experiences not only with students, but also with parents, community members, and other educators. Teachers can also use the app to creatively assign projects or tasks.

Students can use Instagram to capture their learning by taking photos combined with a few words and posting online. This helps the teacher to keep track of the student groups and provide immediate feedback.

Summarizing the Main Points

This section provides readers with a recap of important information covered in the chapter.

- Digital learners prefer just-in-time learning.
- We live in a time of increasingly disposable information.
- Education is modeled around the just-in-case (JiCTL) model of teaching and learning.
- Just-in-time teaching and learning (JiTTL) is a blended instructional approach that uses feedback between classroom activities and work that students do at home in preparation for future classroom activities.
- The goal of the JiTTL model is for students to assume more personal responsibility for the learning process.
- Learners seeking new knowledge in the JiTTL model use tools and sources that are readily available to them. The motivation to learn can be through circumstance like school or learner initiated.

Questions to Consider

Now that you've finished the chapter, consider the following questions.

1. How do you create learning experiences for a world and a new economy that don't yet exist?

2. What's the difference between just-in-time teaching and learning and just-in-case teaching and learning?

3. The JiTTL model requires preparation from both teachers and students prior to attending class. What are your thoughts on this?

4. What is the goal of the JiTTL model?

5. How does the JiTTL model promote engagement?

For up-to-date resource materials
related to this chapter, please visit
http://bit.ly/Attributes_of_Digital_Learners.

Instant Versus Deferred Gratification

The highest reward for a person's toil is not what
they get for it, but what they become by it.

—JOHN RUSKIN

Learning Attribute 7

Digital learners are looking for instant gratification and immediate rewards while simultaneously looking for deferred gratification and delayed rewards. Traditional educational practices have focused on deferred gratification and delayed rewards.

Let us try to explain why we're talking out of both sides of our mouths at the same time. Deferred gratification and delayed rewards say that *if* you study hard, and *if* you keep focused, and *if* you behave, and *if* you attend class regularly, you'll eventually be rewarded with a good letter grade, acceptance to a good school, or the chance for a good job. And we'd like to stress that it's absolutely essential for students to have this kind of focus and discipline.

But at the same time, readers need to understand why digital culture resonates so strongly with these generations. Digital culture provides them with exactly what they need and want the most.

Think back to when we were growing up. Many of us would admit being terribly insecure—and if we were insecure, we constantly looked for affirmation and attention and wanted to be able to distinguish ourselves from others. And we got that attention through academics, athletics, music, social skills, and, for some, even smoking.

It's no different for today's digital generations. They also want constant affirmation, lots of attention, and the ability to distinguish themselves from others. But in addition to academics, sports, or music, the digital generations have embraced gaming, social media, and social media tools as their own.

And there is a payoff for their efforts. Things like smartphones, digital technology, social media tools, and video games all tell users that *if* they put in the hours, and *if* they master the game or tool, they'll be rewarded with the next level, a win, a place on the high scorers' list, or a skill that's respected by their peers. What they *do* determines exactly what they get, and what they *get* is obviously worth the hundreds, if not thousands, of hours of effort they put in to develop these skills.

That's deferred gratification and delayed rewards. New technologies excel at giving deferred gratification and delayed rewards. But at the same time, video games and digital technologies give kids immediate feedback for their efforts and quench their constant thirst for instant gratification. And the payoff for any action is usually extremely clear.

Ian's son Kolby is an internationally renowned 3-D artist who specializes in character and creature creation for video games. He worked for EA Sports and was one of the lead artists in the creation and development of *Mass Effect 2*, one of the world's most popular video games. But he was recruited by Microsoft to go to Seattle and work on the company's blockbuster, top-selling video game *Halo*. Recently, Ian had dinner with Kolby, his wife, and the president of a very successful video game company. The president told Ian that when they create new video games, they intentionally design them to require the players to make a decision every one-half to one second, and they ensure that players are rewarded or punished for those decisions every seven to ten seconds.

A study from the University of Rochester confirms and extends this, suggesting people who play action-based video and computer games are forced to make choices and act on them up to six times a second (Hotz, 2012). That's immediate gratification and instant reward.

But then, the president pulled out his laptop and showed Ian the data that compared how often digital learners were rewarded while playing their games and how often students are asked to make decisions for themselves or are positively rewarded for their actions in the classroom. According to his numbers, on average, students get to ask a question, make a personal decision, or get positively reinforced for their actions in the classroom about once every thirty-five minutes. In fact, the number of minutes is probably much higher than that.

Let's do the math—even if a teacher calls on or acknowledges a student once every five minutes, in a classroom of twenty-five, that means, on average, each student will be called upon, be praised, or receive feedback about once every two hours. This might partially explain why there are so many students in our classrooms today waiting for the video game, or virtual version, of school to go on sale online or at Walmart so they don't have to attend traditional schools anymore.

The question is, How can we incorporate both immediate gratification and immediate rewards and deferred gratifications and delayed rewards into our classroom experiences?

Strategies and Tools That Work

What follows are some examples of learning strategies and web-based tools that help incorporate digital learners' desire for immediate gratification and rewards with deferred gratification and delayed rewards.

ClassDojo: www.classdojo.com

ClassDojo is a classroom management tool that helps teachers improve behavior in their classrooms quickly and easily. Teachers are able to track student behavior and provide instant feedback by displaying each student's name with recognition points. Teachers can share student progress with parents and administrators. ClassDojo promotes better learning behaviors, provides suggestions for smoother lessons, and generates easily accessible data, and best of all, it's free and available for computers, tablets, and smartphones. ClassDojo provides students with instant gratification and immediate reward when they behave properly in class and see it displayed on the teacher's screen. Also, ClassDojo provides deferred gratification and delayed rewards when teachers use the collected behavioral data when issuing grades or conduct codes in school at the end of the quarter, marking period, or academic year. (See figure 10.1, page 112.)

Source: ClassDojo. Used with permission.

Figure 10.1: ClassDojo screenshot.

The Digital Frame

This next strategy is an old feedback practice with a new, digital twist. Most teachers are aware of the time-honored practice of displaying student work on a bulletin board. Digital frames display a revolving selection of digital photographs, which can be uploaded directly from a digital camera or memory card. Digital frames are fairly inexpensive. Teachers and students can capture examples of good student work to display. While a traditional bulletin board may only be able to hold ten or fifteen examples of student work, a digital frame can display hundreds of examples in slide show mode. As teachers observe good student work, they can upload it to the digital frame in a matter of minutes. Students will attempt to earn spots in the frame's revolving slide show of exemplars—providing delayed rewards and deferred gratification. (See figure 10.2.)

Source: Courtesy of Playcraft Malta. Used with permission.

Figure 10.2: Digital frame screenshot.

Digital Game–Based Learning

How many of you have played *Angry Birds*? (Be honest.) What skills can this game, downloaded more than two billion times, teach or demonstrate? The *Angry Birds* franchise has over thirty million unique users logging in monthly—that's one million players a day! (See figure 10.3, page 114.) The game's developer worked with NASA on the microgravity used in *Angry Birds Space* to improve its educational value (if you can ignore the exploding pigs in a vacuum). That collaboration reached a new orbit with the landing of the Mars Curiosity rover and the release the same month of an *Angry Birds Space Red Planet* update with explicit links to NASA educational content about Mars (Dredge, 2012). And what does *Angry Birds* teach students?

- Newton's laws of motion
- Numeration

- Data analysis

- Experimentation

- Trial and error

- Strategic planning

- Parabola

- Trajectory

- Cause and effect

- The scientific method

- Goal commitment

These are just some examples of what the game teaches students. There's even a preschool/kindergarten curriculum based on *Angry Birds* gameplay.

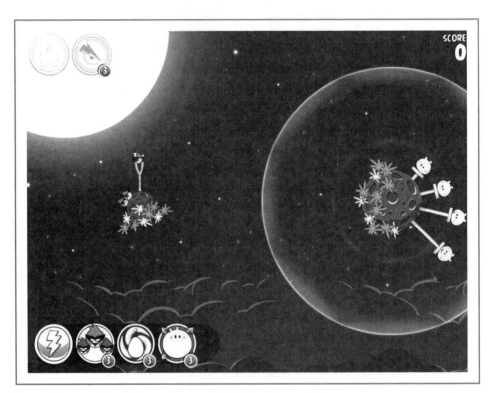

Source: Courtesy of Rovio Entertainment, Ltd. Used with permission.

Figure 10.3: *Angry Birds* screenshot.

How many of you remember *The Oregon Trail*? Your students can experience the next generation of *The Oregon Trail* story. You and your fictitious family can finally settle down and build a new town in the Wild West. *The Oregon Trail: American*

Settler is a fun-filled game stocked with engaging features to keep everyone entertained for hours and hours. In *The Oregon Trail: American Settler*, players:

- Create and manage their own frontier town
- Relive memorable moments from the original game
- Place hundreds of buildings, livestock, and crops
- Customize characters with various outfits
- Play hunting or fishing mini-games for resources
- Face the dangers of the Wild West—stampedes, tornadoes, and more

What can this game teach students? How might you incorporate it into instruction? Let's break down the embedded concepts into subject areas:

- Social studies (history, westward expansion, factors of production, resources, opportunity cost, technology from the past)
- Reading (challenging vocabulary, slang versus formal language, connection with westward expansion novels)
- Math (adding, subtracting large numbers in real-world context, data collection, time management)
- Writing (narratives, persuasive writing)

Many digital games exist that promote opportunities for deep learning across many content areas. Whether used as a lesson warm-up, instructional event, review work, reteaching strategy, assessment, or extension activity, digital games provide students with the ability to learn as they play. And as they play, they are receiving constant rewards and consequences for their actions. Eventually, as they progress through the learning game, they will receive delayed rewards and deferred gratification because games take time to play and can't be rushed.

Digital Badges

Just as badges have demonstrated mastery and accomplishment in the real world, digital badges provide students with a record of their good work. Badges are thought of as rewards and are most effective when used to contribute to setting goals, developing a positive reputation, affirmation of status and skill mastery, completed instruction, and group identification. In keeping with the students' love of bling, awarding them with tangible feedback empowers their intrinsic needs, which is far more powerful (and cheap) than extrinsic ones. Open Badge Designer provides a simple way to layer different shapes and images on top of each other to create an attractive, colorful open badge graphic that can be used to track a student's learning path and provide a cumulative record of student performance. (See figure 10.4 for an example of a digital badge.)

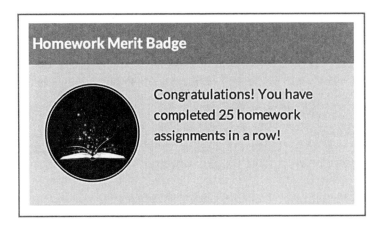

Source: ClassBadges. Used with permission.

Figure 10.4: Example of a digital badge.

Video or Audio Feedback

Traditionally, students receive written or oral feedback. While constructive written feedback can be individualized and specific and offer students points to reflect on, it is typically deferred feedback. After years of receiving feedback in this manner, students may be looking for something more immediate and personal.

Short audio or video clips can be powerful outlets for sharing information related to student progress and performance: "I am less generic and am able to elaborate my points with more passion, precision, and focus than I would ordinarily do in a written piece of feedback" (Hayden, 2014). Google Voice, Skype, Instagram, Kaizena, Evernote, TwitPic via Twitter, or even a video camera on a smartphone can be used to share video comments. With the click of a button, students can quickly have meaningful feedback. They don't have to wait for extended periods of time as they would if the comments were in written form.

Additional Strategies, Apps, and Resources to Explore

In the section that follows, there are some additional apps, resources, and strategies to consider using with students to offer them both instant and deferred gratification as well as immediate and delayed rewards.

Music

For years, educators have been using music and sound to cue students. However, music is also a powerful incentive for students during classwork. During a time when students are working individually or with others, music is used as a reward for beginning and maintaining their workflow. The practice of incorporating music into classroom instruction also has an immediate and deferred impact on the human brain and productivity. Teresa Lesiuk (2005), an associate professor in the music therapy program at the University of Miami, found that "those who listened to music completed their tasks more quickly and came up with better ideas than those who didn't, because the music improved their mood" (Padnani, 2012). Melodious sounds encourage the release of dopamine in the reward area of the brain. Playing music during a classroom activity can be used as a powerful incentive. The music provides students with the instant gratification found in dopamine release, but there is also the strong possibility that students will improve long-term work habits if music is linked to their classroom experiences.

Active Learning

When children are forced to sit idly for long periods of time as they do listening to the teacher talk or preparing for standardized tests, they get "ants in their pants." This instructional practice goes completely against their energy level. Children are Energizer Bunnies! If they sit still and listen without engagement and movement for long periods of time, they will fidget, become easily distracted, and disconnect.

Students must be mentally and physically invested during the learning process. By incorporating movement exercises or workstations in the classroom, teachers are able to channel students' energy into productive, active learning scenarios. Easy strategies include spelling vocabulary with the shape of their bodies, polling students by having them go to a certain area of the room to identify their choices, workstation or carousel brainstorming, and simple movement breaks.

Students will experience the instant gratification and reward of utilizing their pent-up energy for productive and enjoyable learning experiences. They will pay attention, stay on task, and feel more engaged because they prefer to be moving, not always trapped in their seat. By promoting an active, engaging lifestyle for the digital generations, students will also experience deferred gratification, and because they are active, they will become better practitioners of balance in their digital and nondigital lives.

Personal Digital Devices

One of the biggest trends in education today is Bring Your Own Device (BYOD) initiatives, which promote student use of personal digital devices in the classroom. By allowing them to use their own devices for classroom research, communication, and participation, teachers have the opportunity to demonstrate trust by allowing them to learn the way they prefer to learn, which is instantly gratifying and rewarding for students. By allowing them to learn in their preferred manner, educators provide students the opportunity to own their learning—ownership that will be rewarding and gratifying today, tomorrow, and a decade from now.

Positive Texts, Emails, or Phone Calls Home

In the past, the only time teachers called home was for student transgressions. However, by selecting exemplary student work and behavior, teachers can easily share positive news with their students' parents. If the parent is not home or doesn't answer, have the student leave a message as a personalized bonus. They will be thrilled to share the news with their folks. This practice strengthens the school-home connection and will add a sense of importance to the practice as students strive to be the ones receiving a phone call, email, or text home.

Summarizing the Main Points

This section provides readers with a recap of important information covered in the chapter.

- The digital generations seek constant affirmation, lots of attention, and the ability to distinguish themselves from their peers.

- The digital generations have embraced social media and its tools as their own.

- Smartphones, digital technologies, social media tools, and video games tell users that if they put in the hours, and if they master the game or tool, they'll be rewarded with the next level, a win, a place on the high scorers' list, or a skill that's respected by their peers. That's deferred gratification.

- On average, students get to ask a question, make a personal decision, or get positively reinforced for their actions in the classroom about once every thirty-five minutes. Technology systems are constructed to give the user immediate feedback, rewards, or consequences for their actions.

- Many tools, strategies, and approaches highlighted in this chapter are designed to provide instant and deferred gratification, as well as immediate and delayed rewards.

Questions to Consider

Now that you've finished the chapter, consider the following questions.

1. How can we incorporate both immediate gratification and rewards and deferred gratification and delayed rewards into our classroom experiences?

2. Why is it that today's children require so much more instant gratification and rewards compared to previous generations?

3. Why have members of the digital generations flocked to social media with such passion and vigor?

4. Although teachers will never be completely replaced in the learning process, how does technology such as digital games provide instant gratification and immediate rewards in ways and frequencies that humans cannot?

5. What is the payoff for the digital generations when they play video games, use their smartphones, and interact with social media for hours and hours on end?

For up-to-date resource materials
related to this chapter, please visit
http://bit.ly/Attributes_of_Digital_Learners.

Chapter 11

Transfluency

The digital generations use technology as an essential tool to connect to their culture—the use of tools like smartphones is not optional for kids today.

—Ian Jukes

Learning Attribute 8

Many of the digital generations are *transfluent*—their visual-spatial skills are so highly evolved that they appear to have cultivated a complete physical interface between their digital and real worlds. Meanwhile, many traditional educators, not to mention young teachers, continue to struggle with the place and purpose of digital technologies in the classroom.

Because of digital bombardment, many of the digital generations have become completely comfortable using a wide range of media and are able to seamlessly shift between their digital and nondigital worlds. They have completely internalized the use of digital tools and, as a result, take them for granted. For them, the Internet is a natural, transparent space, fully integrated into their lives. The new digital landscape does not exist in isolation from the physical world. In fact, it has become such an internalized part of their lives that many of the digital generations actually live a hybrid existence that seamlessly integrates communication, information, and entertainment with social media to create a world that many of the older generations struggle to understand. The digital generations are transfluent—they are able to jump back and forth between the real world and the digital world with ease, and they are able to seamlessly fit the two worlds together through the use of their digital devices.

Case in point: On May 21, 2014, Michael Jackson, also known as the King of Pop, appeared on the Billboard Music Awards show to sing his new song "Slave to the

Music." What made his performance highly unusual is that it took place almost five years after he tragically lost his life in June 2009. What the audience saw was a virtual representation of Jackson, and—here's the amazing part—many in the audience wouldn't have been able to tell the difference between the real and the virtual Michael Jackson had they not known he was deceased. For those in attendance, the digital landscape didn't exist in isolation from the physical world (Cartier-Wells, 2013).

An even more remarkable example of interaction between real and virtual worlds is anime. Anime is Japanese animated productions, usually featuring hand-drawn or computer animation. Anime culture is extremely popular today with young people all over the world. The productions are full of highly expressive visuals that many viewers find extremely compelling.

This link, www.youtube.com/watch?v=pEaBqiLeCu0 (Immersivetech, 2010), will take you to a YouTube video of an anime concert in Tokyo. Just like any other concert video you might have seen, there are screaming crowds dancing, singing, chanting, and swaying to the music. But this concert is different. The lead singer is Hatsune Miku, a humanoid persona voiced by a singing synthesizer application and projected as a hologram (Verini, 2012).

Now you might be thinking that Hatsune Miku would just be popular in Japan, but her recent world tour included concerts in Los Angeles; Washington, DC; and Minneapolis that played to near-capacity crowds. When we first saw this video, we thought how clever it was that the producers had taken some singer, created a hologram, and added a voice. But Hatsune Miku is a little more complicated than that. You see, there is no Hatsune Miku. Hatsune Miku is just computer music software that enables users to create synthesized singing of unprecedented quality and remarkable realism by simply typing in lyrics and adding melodies created by Yamaha's Vocaloid (Vocal + Android) technology.

Hatsune Miku is a completely digital creation. Anyone using the Yamaha software can quickly compose a Hatsune Miku song and then use related software to create a hologram. In the past few years, there have been almost one million songs and movies created about and by Hatsune Miku posted to YouTube.

This is exactly what we are referring to when we write about digital culture and the connection between the digital world and the real world. Imagine if, instead of Hatsune Miku, the hologram was Albert Einstein talking about black holes, or Nelson Mandela describing how to help a nation overcome apartheid, or Neil

Armstrong discussing his historic landing on the Moon. The possibilities are unlimited.

To the digital generations, their devices are transparent. They are second nature and thus taken for granted. Although the digital generations covet their smartphones and tablets, they don't think about them—the devices are just a means to an end, not an end in itself: "No one gets excited over using a welder, but its ability to connect different pieces together to create something unique and useful from raw material is where its value as a tool really shines" (Cohen, 2014).

The digital generations use their tools to create seamless gateways between real and virtual worlds. They create unique and useful solutions to real-world problems by transforming raw information into new knowledge that they connect to existing knowledge. This is the definition of transfluency.

Strategies and Tools That Work

What follows are some examples of learning strategies and web-based tools that help provide digital learners with a bridge between real and virtual worlds.

Virtual Field Trips

Students enjoy the powerful experience of a field trip. These educational excursions break up the normal rhythm of school routine and provide students with a fresh, new, and enriching learning experience outside of a traditional classroom. Unfortunately, reality sets in for students, parents, and teachers. Such things as travel expenses, reservations, student safety issues, and weather conditions can turn a potentially valuable learning experience into a costly, logistical nightmare.

Instead of taking the students on a field trip, teachers can bring the field trip to the students without the cost and challenges of planning it. With the power of information and communication technologies, students are able to travel to far-off places without ever leaving their classrooms. At its core, a transfluent learning experience intertwines digital and real worlds. A virtual field trip allows participants, independently or collectively, to experience a safe, enriching, low-cost learning adventure.

Virtual field trips utilize interactive websites, multimedia resources, live-feed web cameras, and even classroom visitors and experts to deliver an immersive experience for students that is second only to a real visit to the location. (See figure 11.1, page 124.)

Source: Courtesy of Jean Taylor. Used with permission.

Figure 11.1: Virtual field trip image.

Global Trek: http://teacher.scholastic.com/activities /globaltrek

This adventure from Scholastic looks like the Expedia travel website but is created for students eager to explore the world. Students make their travel choices from an extensive list of countries and maintain a travel journal to chronicle their trip experiences. When students arrive in the country of their choice, they are provided with a travel itinerary that offers background information about the country and its people.

NASA: Ames Research Center—http://quest.nasa.gov/vft

This virtual field trip produced by NASA is an immersive multimedia experience developed to support student exploration of areas on Earth that have been identified as analog sites to regions on Mars. Users are taken from a global view directly down to the ground view of a site. They are placed into a 360-degree panorama of that location. Users navigate around the site, interacting with various objects, as well as scientists they learn from. Each environment consists of a variety of virtual reality experiences, global fly-downs, and video files.

Colonial Williamsburg

Colonial Williamsburg (www.history.org/history/teaching/eft/explore.cfm) is an example of one of the best virtual field trips out there. Its Emmy Award–winning real-time Internet events integrate live broadcasts, video-on-demand, and contact with content experts and instructional resources for teachers.

Welcome to Bayville

The Welcome to Bayville site (http://bayville.thinkport.org/default_flash.aspx) offers seven interactive activities that will help students, teachers, and families learn more about the Chesapeake Bay area—the largest estuary in the United States.

Smithsonian National Museum of Natural History

This comprehensive tour (www.mnh.si.edu/panoramas) allows visitors to take a virtual, self-guided, room-by-room walking tour of the entire museum.

Augmented Reality

Have you ever seen the films *The Terminator*, *RoboCop*, and *Iron Man*? Whether a villain or hero, the movie characters used data, sensors, and heads-up displays to give themselves a real-time advantage over their adversaries. In essence, their reality was augmented by real-time data.

Augmented reality (AR) is a way of combining the real and virtual worlds together by overlaying digital data onto real-world analog views, effectively blurring the line between the digital and corporeal world.

Teachers will never have the big budget of the movie studios (or Iron Man's Stark Industries), but the data provide people with a heightened awareness of reality. Humans are born with five senses, but technology enhances our perceptions. It provides a clearer picture by streaming additional information our traditional senses might have missed.

Many professions now, or in the future, will depend on augmented reality. Some of these professions include doctors, nurses, aircraft pilots, and military personnel. People even use AR apps to search for jobs by pointing their phones at a building to see the job openings available inside.

In the classroom, AR can help add connections between what students see and don't see. Take, for instance, a narrative students read in class. The reader is aware of all the characters and their dialogue, thoughts, and secrets. AR awareness can help tell the story of what is going on through human senses and a technological interface.

FETCH! Lunch Rush (Ages 4+)

Produced by PBS Kids through a U.S. Department of Education grant, Fetch! Lunch Rush (https://itunes.apple.com/us/app/fetch!-lunch-rush/id469089331?mt=8) is an AR game that uses printed cards and a story line to provide players with a digitally enhanced, mathematical scavenger hunt using real-world interaction with numbers.

Augmented Reality Solar System (Content Rating: Everyone)

This app (https://itunes.apple.com/us/app/ar-solar-system/id779879932?mt=8?) provides an interactive tour of the solar system using cool graphics and actual NASA data. In Apple's App Store, a similar app named SolAR System Discovery is available (https://itunes.apple.com/us/app/solar-system-discovery/id485333158?mt=8).

Geocaching

Geocaching is a recreational activity where participants use a global positioning system (GPS) receiver or other mobile device and navigational techniques to hide and locate containers, called "geocaches" or "caches," anywhere in the world. (See figure 11.2 for images of geocaching.)

Source: J.D. Meyers. Used with permission.

Figure 11.2: Geocaching images.

The applications for classroom use are nearly endless. Burt Lo (2010), author of *GPS and Geocaching in Education*, identifies numerous classroom applications for geocaching. Teachers must start with these questions in mind before undertaking this exciting endeavor.

Do you want this activity primarily to:

- Guide student learning about the larger world? (geography, geology, ecology, history, and so on)

- Make abstract concepts real? (mathematics, physics, chemistry)

- Help students improve logic and problem-solving skills? (solving puzzles, finding caches)

- Practice community etiquette and promote small-group work? (online and in the real world)

- Provide focus for writing and art assignments? (posting online, creating signature items) (Lo, 2010, p. 99)

Geocaching excursions provide students with hands-on, brains-on activities that can easily cater to a wide range of learning experiences. Students leave the confines of their two-by-four-by-six classroom (two covers of the textbook, four walls of the classroom, and six periods a day) to explore and solve problems independently or in teams. Many geocaching apps exist, so teachers can develop and facilitate engaging and relevant explorative tasks, while students utilize their mobile devices to participate.

The Geocaching (www.geocaching.com/live/default.aspx) website provides access to more than two million geocaching adventures and six million active geocachers around the world. In fact, there's probably one nearby right now! The site also has an App Store, Google Play, and Windows Phone app for download.

Another awesome geocaching service is Munzee (www.munzee.com/download). Munzee is a real-world, real-time scavenger hunt game where items are discovered and captured using a smartphone. Players work through multiple levels and gain rankings based on scores. Points are obtained by capturing other players' Munzees or when your deployed Munzees are captured by other players. The site also has an App Store, Google Play, and Windows Phone app for download.

Edmodo: www.edmodo.com

Similar to Facebook, Edmodo is a social networking service that allows students to connect with one another to collaborate on learning tasks. It also provides teachers with useful tools to measure student progress and personalize the learning experience. Unlike Facebook, Edmodo is *exclusively* geared toward education and is generally safer than at-large, public social networking services. Teachers take on the roles of facilitators and host their students online as a means to foster productive, collaborative online learning communities. As an added bonus, parents are able to take part in the online learning environment, albeit in a limited fashion.

Teachers can conduct and moderate online discussions with their students; construct and dispense polls to receive student feedback; distribute documents, hyperlinks, videos, images, and other resources for student use; and recognize good behavior with an incentive-based digital badge system.

Student performance and participation are easily measured in numerous ways. Traditional assessment methods such as quizzes and assignments are easily created, disseminated, and scored using the social networking platform. Edmodo also tracks performance benchmarks such as digital reward badges. Teachers are able to use Edmodo's metrics for data analysis to monitor student successes and failures and react accordingly.

Edmodo is also a valuable tool for professional development. Teachers are able to connect using the social network to share resources and instructional strategies to improve instruction and benefit their global professional learning communities.

Google Hangouts

As part of the Google+ experience, Google Hangouts allow users to video chat with one person or up to ten people simultaneously. Hangout sessions can be shared and archived easily, capturing the media-rich discussions for later use. Hangout participants can share resources, computer screens, and conversations using other Google services such as Google Drive, YouTube, Google Search, Google Maps, and Picasa Web Albums.

In essence, Google Hangouts provide users with free videoconferencing experiences that are easily shared with others. This innovative form of learning breaks down the traditional barriers of formalized classroom learning and leverages the power of collaborative experiences using digital technologies. Be mindful of distance learning challenges such as time zone differences and potential bandwidth limitations.

To see a demo of Google Hangouts in action, please visit www.google.com/+ /learnmore/hangouts.

Additional Strategies, Apps, and Resources to Explore

What follows is a section with more strategies, apps, and resources to consider using with the always-on generation.

Blackboard Collaborate

Blackboard Collaborate (www.blackboard.com/platforms/collaborate/overview.aspx) is an interactive platform providing virtual meeting spaces and tools to conduct online trainings, meetings, and classes.

EarthCam: www.earthcam.com

EarthCam provides thousands of live web camera feeds from hundreds of locations around the globe.

Second Life: http://secondlife.com

Second Life is a vast, multilayered, complex, and sophisticated virtual world where participants create and operate their own personal avatars and interact with others in environments where they can buy land, build structures, converse, and attend classes on a digital campus where they can earn real undergraduate and graduate degrees.

Tellagami: https://tellagami.com

Tellagami is a mobile app that lets you create and share a quick animated video called a Gami. The app allows users to create and customize an avatar that will record and speak a message in your own voice or type messages for a synthesized voice to say.

Summarizing the Main Points

This section provides readers with a recap of important information covered in the chapter.

- Due to chronic digital bombardment, many of the digital generations are completely comfortable using a wide range of media and seamlessly shift between digital and nondigital worlds.

- Many of the digital generations actually live a hybrid existence and effortlessly integrate communication, information, entertainment, and social media with their nondigital lives.

- For many in the digital generations, the digital landscape doesn't exist in isolation from the physical world.

- To the digital generations, their devices are transparent—they are just a means to an end.

- The digital generations use their tools to create gateways between real and virtual worlds. They create unique and useful solutions to real-world problems by transforming raw information into new knowledge that they connect to existing knowledge. This is the definition of *transfluency*.

Questions to Consider

Now that you've finished the chapter, consider the following questions.

1. What is transfluency?

2. Why do many of the older generations struggle to understand the digital generations' need to exist in both digital and nondigital worlds?

3. What are the tools and services that the digital generations use to create this hybrid existence?

4. How do the digital generations view their digital devices?

5. How can the digital generations prosper in both their digital and nondigital realities?

For up-to-date resource materials related to this chapter, please visit http://bit.ly/Attributes_of_Digital_Learners.

Chapter 12

Learning Must Be Fun

From learning by listening to learning by doing . . . education and learning will become as much fun as video games.

—Bing Gordon

Learning Attribute 9

Digital learners prefer learning that is simultaneously relevant, engaging, active, instantly useful, and fun. Many educators are compelled to teach memorization of the primarily content-based material in the curriculum guide to prepare students for the standardized tests they regularly have to face. This is happening at the expense of cultivating the higher-order thinking skills and new basic skills for the 21st century all students will need to have once they leave school.

The digital generations are frequently criticized, derided, misunderstood, misrepresented, and disrespected in the press. They are often accused of being intellectual slackers and antisocial human beings who lack even basic social skills. This is generational slander. danah boyd (2014) and our own personal experiences say that on the contrary, for the vast majority of the digital generations, the digital world is far from an isolating experience.

Outside of school, students are hyperconnected, linked continuously to others in a global intelligence. They're immersed in virtual environments based on a participatory culture that allows them to interact not only with their classmates, but also with people who are not geographically close. Not long ago, this kind of instant communication was literally and figuratively impossible.

They are a highly social generation. Here's the difference—they use methods and tools the older generations did not have around when they were growing up. The always-on generation live at least part of the time in digital worlds they've created for themselves. They play *Minecraft*, they play *Mass Effect*, they play *Halo*, they play *Angry Birds*—they play hundreds of other games that are exciting and engaging. And they use digital tools to constantly stay connected to everyone and everything.

And in these virtual environments, they create and control everything. They are users. They are active. There is excitement, novelty, risk, and the company of peers. It's somewhere they can turn for advice and information. They observe, they inquire, they participate, they discuss, they argue, they play, they critique, and they investigate. Digital technologies engage the digital generations in ways that are relevant to their lives, allowing them to learn by doing as they experiment with new social and cultural realms. The digital generations don't need a user's manual or human being to teach them how to play the latest video game, learn an app, or use a new digital device. They like to explore things for themselves and take personal control of their own learning. For many students, this may be the first experience of empowerment in their lives, enabling them to be heard, counted, and taken seriously. Personal experience and observation show us that students learn best when they are in control of their own learning.

As a result, it's not surprising that the digital generations can become easily frustrated because many of them have a digital life outside of school and a nondigital life in school. Increasingly, they expect—in fact, demand—to own the learning and to be in control at least part of the time.

The problem is that what they expect and regularly experience in the world outside of school with their games and devices and texting and websites is often completely at odds with what they experience in the classroom. After they have spent hundreds, if not thousands, of hours of their lives engaged in virtual environments, they come to school where almost everything is controlled by adults. They are compelled to sit in classrooms where things are hierarchical and unidirectional—where the teacher stands at the front of the room talking at them nonstop without even using visuals.

The digital generations tell us this is boring. They control nothing. They have to sit there passively and listen. For them, school is all about being passive observers and learning endless deferred gratification.

We can absolutely assure you that it will not be possible for very much longer to engage young people in an educational system where the quality of the experiences school provides are not as inviting and engaging as the quality of the experiences they can get outside of school. The traditional classroom is no longer enough for them.

Education's challenge is to keep up. The digital generations will never accept the traditional stand-and-deliver educational model. They need to be in a situation where they're controlling things at least part of the time, and that can never happen in the current school environment with education's traditional mindsets toward teaching, learning, and assessment.

Why is it that young kids can solve the most complex problems in a video game involving strategic thinking, critical analysis, and immediate decision making, yet there continues to be a disconnect between the skills they demonstrate outside of schools and the skills they are asked to draw on inside of school?

Right beneath our personal radar, digital learners are very much an intellectual, problem-solving, and highly social generation. They have highly developed critical thinking, problem-solving, and social skills. The problem is that their social skills and their problem-solving skills are just not the skills that the older generations value. Nor are these the skills that are typically tested for in schools today. So their extraordinary cognitive and technical abilities are simply not acknowledged or are dismissed.

Now, there are some experts who argue that the experiences the digital generations are having, and the skills they're developing, are worthless, time-wasting, and irrelevant to education. It has taken us years to realize that play and games are simply preparation for work and life after school. What we now understand is that for today's digital generations, play *is* work, and work is increasingly seen in terms of games and gameplay. That's why the digital generations want their learning to be relevant, instantly useful, fun, and engaging. But beyond this, more than anything else, when it comes to their learning, the digital generations want to know the answer to two simple questions: Why in the world am I learning this? And what possible connection does this have to me and my world?

And for the digital generations, the correct answers are not because it might be on the test or needed to pass the course. That's just not enough reason for them.

Because of digital bombardment, the younger generations' brains have been completely saturated with information and digital technology, so their brains are physically different from ours. And as a result, they think and process information differently, using different parts of the brain differently than people of our generations do. And it doesn't stop there. Kids four, three, even two years apart are having completely different experiences with their technologies. In fact, we're beginning to see accelerated differences in the brains of the younger generations—between the brains of teenagers, tweenagers, and younger children. This constantly changing brain is a result of chronic digital bombardment that is an everyday part of their lives.

For the digital generations, it's become love at first swipe. Many of them learn to type before they learn to write, and they use a keyboard more than they use a pen. Anyone who has seen a toddler playing with a tablet knows exactly what we're talking about. Technology is not new if you were born into it. To a young child, a magazine is just a tablet that doesn't work. Based on the way digital technologies are emerging today, we have to understand that a tablet may be the most primitive technology they will ever use.

How profoundly have children been affected by the new digital landscape? According to a Cisco Systems (2006) survey, 70 percent of children between the ages of two and five can operate a computer mouse or a trackpad, but only 11 percent of them can tie their own shoes.

Now, there is much more we could say here, but we hope this brief overview explains at least in part why kids act differently, why they behave the way they do, why they respond to the world the way they do, why they learn the way they do, how they view the world, and what interests and engages them. And this might help, at least in part, explain some of the fundamental differences between their generations and ours.

Yet sadly—and this is what frustrates us more than anything—there is no other industry that ignores research in its own field the way education has. Education stands alone in the disconnect between what it knows and what it does. Currently, there is little relationship in a classroom between how children learn and how teachers teach. Despite the fact that we have decades of research on what really works in the classroom (and what doesn't work), almost nothing of what we have learned about how our children's brains and minds function is being applied in classrooms today.

New technologies have changed everything, but very few people in education really get that since there are very few people in education under the age of twenty-five. So we just have to ask this question: "If kids are way ahead of teachers in developing the skills needed to succeed in the digital world of the future, and if many teachers are completely unaware of the significance of the skills kids have developed in this digital world, and if teachers continue to do things in the classroom that we already know don't work [because we do], then who here really has the learning problem? Is it the kids, or is it us?"

We think that there's great irony in the fact that many experienced teachers are struggling trying to become learners and leaders in the new digital landscape. It's a great challenge to unlearn being a traditional teacher.

What's the definition of insanity? It's doing things the same way we have always done them but expecting, or wanting, or needing completely different results. But if we continue to do what we have always done, we'll continue to get what we've always got. And in doing so, we'll fail our children and fail our nation.

Strategies and Tools That Work

What follows are some examples of learning strategies and web-based tools that help address digital learners' need for learning to be fun.

20% Time

Originally adopted by Google, 20% Time is a strategy that allows Google employees to spend 20 percent of their working time exploring personal interests outside of their assigned duties. In schools, this would mean allowing students to explore their own interests and follow their natural curiosity 20 percent of the time. 20% Time translates into setting aside time for one activity in a lesson, one lesson in a unit, or one unit in a term for self-determined and self-directed student exploration.

> What 20% time allows students to do is pick their own project and learning outcomes, while still hitting all the standards and skills for their grade level. In fact, these students often go "above and beyond" their standards by reaching for a greater depth of knowledge than most curriculum tends to allow. (Juliani, 2013)

At first glance, this might seem to be instructional chaos. However, teachers, acting as guides or facilitators, help the students make their projects and interests connect with the standards. For example, if a student is passionate about studying sharks, then the teacher provides the student with an opportunity to study sharks and create a shark documentary. In this quick scenario, students must research, write an expository script, and produce a multimedia product. If you are keeping count, students are reading, performing research, doing expository writing, speaking, and creating a multimedia product. All these are completed by allowing students 20 percent of instructional time to study what they are passionate about.

This may seem at first glance to be a tall order. Educators handing over control of students' learning and allowing them to explore whatever subjects they want runs completely contrary to traditional educational assumptions about teaching, learning, and assessment. Jumping completely into this approach without proper preparation would be highly disorienting for both students and teachers alike, because both have learned early on how to play the game called school.

Teachers are completely comfortable standing at the front of the room and teaching. Students quickly learn that they're supposed to sit still, pay attention, and follow instructions. If the 20% Time model is going to be successful, we must start by slowly providing students with more and more personal responsibility for their learning by progressively shifting the burden for the learning from the teacher to the student, where it belongs. This is also a great way to slowly begin to make the shift from traditional teaching and learning to a more problem-based model.

Picking Their Product

Picking their product is an approach that allows students the opportunity to select the form of their final product. Although the teacher maintains all the same expectations for each potential product, students are left with the freedom to select the medium the product will be displayed in.

If a class has just completed a unit exploring westward expansion, then students have the choice of creating a play, constructing an informative poster, creating a short video or presentation, developing a board game, or any other means of demonstrating their understanding of standards or key curricular concepts.

Digital Gaming

Using digital games in the classroom puts the power of learning in the hands of students and promotes a student-centered approach to teaching, learning, and assessment. Digital games compel teachers to step out of the spotlight and become facilitators of learning, rather than the gatekeepers of all information. (See figure 12.1 for an example of a digital game, *Sandbox EDU*.) Students today prefer not to be lectured at. They want to receive information from multiple sources and like to generate their own knowledge from the readily available resources (digital and traditional) that are all around them. The critical step in using digital gaming in the classroom is to identify an appropriate game that aligns well with the concepts to be explored as outlined in the curriculum.

> The experiences become more meaningful as the students create the learning and assume ownership of the newly acquired knowledge. This approach will prove to be a significant change for many teachers, as it is a paradigm shift from the traditional approaches to skills and learning they have been using in the classroom on a daily basis. (Schaaf & Mohan, 2014, p. 8)

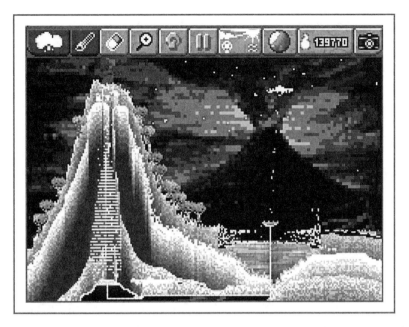

Source: The Sandbox EDU *game by Pixowl is available at www.thesandboxgame.com/education. Used with permission.*

Figure 12.1: The *Sandbox EDU* game.

Scenario-Based Learning

Curriculum is often introduced without a context to help the learner understand the relevancy of what is being taught. Concepts taught in isolation from context will only irregularly be retained.

> Scenario-based learning (SBL) uses interactive scenarios to support active learning strategies such as problem-based or case-based learning. It normally involves students working their way through a storyline, usually based around an ill-structured or complex problem, which they are required to solve. (National Centre for Teaching and Learning of Massey University, n.d.)

In the SBL process, students must use their own knowledge and the new basics to develop real-world, real-time solutions to real-world problems or simulations of those problems. A scenario might begin with a prompt such as:

> Allison is driving with her parents when they get in a serious car accident. At the emergency room, the doctor tells Allison that her mother is fine, but her father Bob has lost a lot of blood and will need a blood transfusion. Allison volunteers to donate blood, and you tell her that her blood type is AB. Bob is type O.

1. Can Allison donate blood to Bob? Why or why not?

2. Allison, who is a biology student, begins to wonder if she is adopted. What would you tell her and why? (Novak, 2014)

Using scenarios such as this, students are challenged to explore, interpret, and apply key curricular concepts as a catalyst for active learning. By linking curricular concepts and processes to authentic, personally relevant tasks, students are able to make the connection to the embedded content.

Homework Makeover

Homework has been a staple in the school-home connection for as long as anyone can remember. It provides the opportunity for parents to actively participate in the instruction of their children. However, homework can be dull, repetitive, and mundane, and lack creativity. Oftentimes, students arrive home with a worksheet to complete but with very little idea how to complete it. When students perform this same type of homework 180-plus days a year, homework quickly becomes just another boring task to complete—one that has very little real connection to classroom learning.

Educators need to generate a list of useful, relevant, engaging homework strategies that they can utilize with students to support alternative learning experiences. These strategies should focus on the intended learning, be short in duration, and provide an opportunity for parental participation.

For spelling, use different materials or media to practice vocabulary words. Have the students use lengths of yarn, straws, a stick in sand, or even the student's own body to spell out words. For math, have students identify ways that math is used outside of the classroom. If they are studying subtraction, encourage students to use household items to demonstrate the process of subtraction to parents. Although the digital divide still exists for some, more and more homes are equipped with a computer and Internet connection, and there are a wealth of free websites waiting for parents, students, and teachers to tap into that support this approach.

Finally, provide students with a choice in the homework they complete. This will help them develop a sense of ownership for the work they do. For example, the teacher could brainstorm five homework activities for the week and let students choose three. This way, students are required to do their homework, but have a choice as to the activities they complete. When students feel they have ownership of their learning, they will be inspired and motivated to complete their tasks.

Additional Strategies, Apps, and Resources to Explore

What follows is a section with more strategies, apps, and resources to consider using with the always-on generation.

The Outside Classroom

In his book *Last Child in the Woods*, children's advocate Richard Louv (2008) shares his groundbreaking research identifying the important connection between humans and nature. He concludes that exposure to nature is essential for healthy childhood development and for the physical and emotional health of children and adults alike. He also links the lack of nature in the lives of today's wired generation—what he calls a nature deficit—to some of the most disturbing childhood trends, such as the rise in obesity, attention disorders, and depression.

Some simple and pragmatic instructional strategies and programs that increase the amount of time outside but are still connected to curricular content areas include:

- Creating a butterfly or herb garden
- Having a school grounds cleanup day
- Developing a wetland area
- Creating a composting station
- Participating in a nature walk and recording the experience in a science journal
- Holding outdoor reading time
- Participating in outdoor learning games

Play-Based Learning

Similar to game-based learning (GBL) and digital game–based learning (DGBL), play-based learning (PBL) is a strategy describing the way kids explore and make sense of their worlds. Kids learn to use their brains in different ways to understand and solve problems. Through play-based learning, children develop an understanding of the social and physical conditions that define their world, and the language, symbols, and materials that are used to engage and interact with it.

For this model to be effective, students must have access to areas they can plan, design, construct, or perform in. Learning centers or stations are the easiest method to facilitate this strategy. Although this approach is primarily geared toward younger learners, it can also be modified for older students. A popular strategy is to create a "green screen" area in a corner of the classroom for production and postproduction of student-created movies. Educators have been using play-based learning for decades, because students excel at learning through play.

Act It Out

Role playing is a powerful and versatile active learning strategy for learners of all ages. It is a natural vehicle for learning and provides an authentic method for students to demonstrate their understanding of content, while also engaging the participants and observers in speaking, presenting, and listening (Blatner, 2009). Teachers provide real-world scenarios or prompts that students use to underpin their academic focus, facilitate project planning and preparation, and evaluate performances. As a form of simulated learning, role playing is a highly adaptable approach that fits into most content subjects and grade levels. As a method to demonstrate higher-order thinking skills, role playing is also a great way to encourage students to socialize and work collaboratively in a team.

Summarizing the Main Points

This section provides readers with a recap of important information covered in the chapter.

- Members of the digital generations are often accused of being intellectual slackers and antisocial human beings who lack social skills. This is far from the truth.

- The digital generations are hyperconnected and linked constantly to others in a form of global intelligence. They are a part of a participatory culture that allows them to interact not only with their classmates, but also with people who are not geographically close.

- The digital generations want to be in control of their learning at least part of the time.

- Technology is the essential tool of the 21st century student. These learners prefer to use their devices for meaningful activities but are often required to turn them off once they enter the classroom.

- Many traditional teachers struggle to unlearn the old ways of doing things. They must be prepared to constantly learn, unlearn, and relearn in the same way that the digital generations will need to do in the future.

- The strategies, apps, and resources listed in this chapter give students more freedom—a say in how they learn, what tools they use to learn, and how they demonstrate what they have learned.

Questions to Consider

Now that you've finished the chapter, consider the following questions.

1. Why are the digital generations labeled as intellectual slackers and antisocial creatures by some?

2. How have digital devices and social media transformed the ways the digital generations prefer to communicate with one another?

3. Why is it that young kids can solve complex problems in a video game, but these problem-solving skills do not always transfer to the classroom setting?

4. Is it the digital generations or the educators that must change their ways and embrace the new tools and methods of learning, and *how* must they change?

5. How can educators shift responsibility for learning from the teacher to the student?

For up-to-date resource materials
related to this chapter, please visit
http://bit.ly/Attributes_of_Digital_Learners.

Chapter 13

Time for a Change

We do not need to improve schools, we need to reinvent them for our times. We need people who can think like children.

—SUGATA MITRA

We regularly hear complaints from teachers, parents, and the media about how different kids are today, how differently they learn, and how differently they're motivated. We hear criticisms that kids today can't concentrate the same way the older generations can. We hear that kids today can't even memorize the names of the states, the provinces, or their capitals. And yet, despite the complaints about what kids today can't do, we continue to teach and test them the same way we always have.

A Need for Relevancy

Meanwhile, those same kids are thinking to themselves, "Why in the world do I have to remember the names of the states or the capitals when I can just use Siri or Google and get the answer in three seconds on my smartphone?" At the same time, many teachers are saying, "What's a Siri?" And yet, the same kids who seem completely incapable of remembering the names of the states or the capitals can instantly and with enthusiasm tell you the lyrics of one thousand songs or the attributes of one hundred game characters.

Sir Ken Robinson (2013) likes to point out that the digital generations are living in the most intensely stimulating period in history. They are being besieged with information and having their attention drawn by every platform—from computers to smartphones to tablets to advertising to hundreds of television channels—and then they are getting penalized for getting distracted.

What Is Distracting Them?

What is it that's distracting them? For the most part, it's the boring stuff they're exposed to in school. It's likely no coincidence that the increased diagnoses of attention deficit disorder (ADD) and attention deficit hyperactivity disorder (ADHD) has happened in parallel with the increased emphasis on standardized testing. Miller (2013) examines the incredible discrepancy in reported ADHD diagnoses across different regions of the United States. Stephen Hinshaw, a clinical psychologist, and Richard Scheffler, a health economist, find:

> [There is] a correlation between the states with the highest rates of ADHD diagnosis and laws that penalize school districts when students fail. Some of these laws are what they call "consequential accountability statutes"—that is, laws like No Child Left Behind, which make school funding contingent on the number of students who pass standardized tests. Another kind of accountability law passed by many states requires exams for high school seniors to qualify for graduation. (Miller, 2013)

Kids are being prescribed Ritalin and Adderall—which some describe as dangerous and addictive medications with powerful side effects—as routinely as older generations had their tonsils taken out when they were kids.

From what we read and hear, it would be easy to assume that ADD and ADHD are modern epidemics. The plagues of ADD and ADHD have become the official brain syndromes for the information age and often the standard reason given for why kids are increasingly disengaged from schools and learning. This is not to say that there is no such thing as ADD or ADHD; we are not qualified to say whether there are or aren't such disorders. There are a great many psychologists and pediatricians who think they exist, but it is still a matter for research and discussion. But without question, what's happening is not an epidemic.

From the hundreds of in-depth interviews we've had with members of the digital generations, we can assure you that the vast majority of them aren't disabled—they're just different. In the same way that we were affected by the world we grew up in, so too have the digital generations been affected by the world they are growing up in. That world is very different from the world that we experienced as children. Like us, the digital generations have a cultural brain—a brain that reflects the culture they are living in and the experiences they are having. As a result, the digital generations have a great deal of difficulty identifying with our world and our ways—and as a consequence, they are just not interested. They have no more patience for old ways of teaching and learning than we did when we were growing up, so increasingly they're shutting the older generations out.

Is this really a surprise? Blaming the digital generations for acting the way they do is like blaming a bank for being robbed. If we make students do hour after hour of low-grade clerical work, it shouldn't be surprising that they start to fidget. As Sir Ken Robinson (2013) says, "Children are not, for the most part, suffering from a psychological condition. They're suffering from childhood."

The digital generations are experiencing a world that is increasingly, some might say completely, out of sync with our traditional approaches toward teaching, learning, and assessment. The reality is that many children today do not learn the way teachers prefer to teach. The challenge is that many educators and decision makers just don't get it or aren't willing to acknowledge that there is a widening gap between the world we grew up in, the world we live in today, and the schools we have created. Schools are changing. The challenge we face is that the world is changing many times faster.

In the new digital landscape, our role as educators is not just to stand up in front of our students and show them how smart we are. Rather, it's to help them understand how smart *they* are, foster the new basic skills that will allow them to learn how to learn, and encourage them to take increasing control and responsibility for their own learning.

To be effective 21st century teachers, we must first possess the new basic skills our students are increasingly expected to have as the minimum requirement for survival in the culture of the 21st century. Learning is far more about *headware* than it is about *hardware*. The content learned in a classroom will come and go. Students may or may not remember what has been taught (probably not). Only the processes remain behind in times of radical change. Learning is all about *headware*—critical thinking, problem solving, creativity, and collaboration.

So where do we begin? Anybody who knows anything about learning knows that the secret to success in the classroom has very little to do with being a good disciplinarian or classroom manager and everything to do with creating an engaging methodology that compels students to *want* to be there. Students learn best by personally experiencing learning that is physical, emotional, intellectual, and spiritual. Great teachers provide experiences that create long-term memories and connections. Great teachers engineer learning experiences that maneuver the students into the driver's seat and then the teachers get out of the way (Johnson, 2013).

This is not about *making* students learn; it's about getting students to *want* to learn. Without motivation, there will be no learning. Answer this question: Would students choose to be in your classroom if they didn't have to be there?

Technology in and of itself does not make an educational experience engaging. A teacher is, without question, the best one-to-one device in the classroom. The killer app for the 21st century is a great teacher—a teacher who has a love of learning; a teacher who has an appreciation of the aesthetic, the esoteric, the ethical, and the moral; a teacher who understands the great educational theorists such as Bloom, Gardner, Dewey, Freire, Vygotsky, and Piaget; a teacher who knows how different kids learn at different stages of their lives.

What many people are not willing to acknowledge or accept is that today's learners are not the same learners that schools were originally designed for. And today's learners are certainly not the learners that many of today's educators were trained to teach. It's crazy to think that more than a decade into the 21st century, we're still debating what 21st century learning looks like. Education continues to operate on assumptions about teaching, learning, and assessment that are targeted at students from another age—one that has long passed us by.

As a result, when we travel nationally and internationally, we're increasingly becoming concerned that we're trying to fit square-peg students into round-hole schools, and round-peg students into square-peg schools. And increasingly, we're depending on traditional standardized tests to measure increasingly nonstandardized brains.

We want to be clear that this is not about throwing out traditional educational approaches. There's absolutely a place for traditional teaching, learning, and assessment. There's absolutely a place for basic skills and memorization. There's absolutely a place for traditional education. That's how you transmit culture—that's how you transmit democracy from one generation to the next. And educators have *every right* to expect our students to respect and honor those traditions. Make sure you heard us say that.

But at the same time, we have to understand that the world has fundamentally changed and continues to change at a faster and faster rate. So in the same way that we have *every right* to expect the digital generations to respect, understand, and engage with our world and our values, we absolutely also need to take the time and effort to respect, understand, and engage with their world and their values. And we ignore their world at our peril. What we desperately need is *balance* between our world and theirs—between traditional and digital learning environments.

As you finish this book, the fundamental question to ask yourself is "How have I modified my instructional assumptions and practices to address the fact that kids have fundamentally changed and continue to change?" There's nothing stopping us from changing the way we learn and how we teach. But if you or your colleagues haven't changed markedly in the past ten years, you and they are just not meeting the needs of your students.

And yes, we understand that change is hard. We know that many educators are struggling trying to come to terms with the digital generations and the new digital landscape. But what's happening to the older generations is normal. Every generation since the time of Socrates and Plato, including our parents, has looked at the next generation and said, "What's wrong with kids today?"

There's nothing wrong with them! They're just different. They're neurologically different. That's why they see the world differently. That's why they engage with the world differently.

The Invisible Gorilla

If you have ever attended one of our presentations, you know that we like to finish things with a short video that tests the audience's level of change awareness. We show a video that involves six students—three students wearing white T-shirts and three students wearing black T-shirts. Each group of students has a basketball that students pass back and forth. The audience's task is to count the number of completed passes made in thirty seconds between the students wearing the white T-shirts. The challenge is that the students are moving around fairly quickly, so counting the number of passes is a complex task. At the last minute before we show the video, we tell the audience that there's a very significant gender difference between men and women when it comes to making this count. Then we show them the video (Simons, 2010).

Once the video is finished, we ask the audience to call out how many passes were made between the white-shirted students. Inevitably the numbers are all over the place: fifteen, sixteen, and in one case eighty-two. Then we ask the audience if anyone saw anything unusual happen. Invariably only a few people will put up their hands.

Then we show the audience the same video again. Before we do, we ask them the second time around *not* to count the number of passes but to just watch globally what's going on and see if they notice anything different happening. To the absolute shock and disbelief of many of the people in the audience, halfway through the video, a large ape walks across the stage, turns, and beats its chest, then walks off the other side. We then ask the audience how they possibly could not have seen the ape the first time they viewed the video.

This video is from what is widely known as the Invisible Gorilla research. It was conducted at the University of Illinois by Daniel Simons (2010). What happened to the viewers is what is called perceptual blindness. *Perceptual blindness* happens when we miss something obvious like a large ape walking across a screen, turning and beating its chest, then walking off the other side. We then explain why so many viewers completely missed the ape the first time through.

Figure 13.1: The invisible gorilla.

Cognitively, the audience was primed to look for something specific. They were primed by being given a specific task. They were asked to count the number of passes between the white-shirted students. Then at the very last moment (and this was intentional), we upped the ante by telling the audience that there was a gender difference between men and women, which of course there wasn't. And when we did this, we created a huge problem in their brains.

Here's what happened. If viewers don't have a specific frame of reference for something, it's more than just confusing to them—more than just confusing to their brains. In fact, our brains are conditioned to refuse to see things. In other words, if you're not expecting to see something, you literally won't see it, even if it's standing right in front of you beating its chest.

And that's the real story of this book. This book is about learners who look at the world differently than we do. How many important things are going on in your lives, with your partners, with your children, with your families and friends, and in your communities that you're just not seeing because you're just not paying attention?

In the same way, how many important things are going on in our classrooms with our students that we're missing because we're focused elsewhere? How many things are we missing because we're focused on the short-term: standards, testing, and meeting the curriculum requirements of getting our students ready for the next test, the next topic, the next term, the next level, or the next grade? If we can't see a large gorilla walk across the screen and turn and beat its chest, how many other important things are we missing in our students' lives because we're just not looking for them?

Where Do We Go From Here?

We would like you to finish this book with a moment of stillness. Close your eyes for a moment and reflect on what you have learned reading this book. What is going on in your students' lives? What is going on in your professional life? What is going on in your personal life? What is going on in the lives of those who are closest to you? That's what we'd like you to take away from this book—an understanding that we face a different kind of student, a student who looks at the world in a fundamentally different way than we do.

There are three reasons why organizations and individuals fail. It's either because they are unaware of the changes that are going on around them, they are unwilling to respond to those changes, or they are so mired in tradition that they are simply unable to change. Our hope is that this book has addressed the first obstacle because now you're aware of what is happening in the world outside of education and why it is so critical that you respond. So the question is, Are you willing and able to make the necessary changes? If so, then now is the time to start.

Summarizing the Main Points

This section provides readers with a recap of important information covered in the chapter.

- The digital generations are living in the most intensely stimulating period in history. They are being besieged with information and having their attention drawn by every platform—from computers to smartphones to tablets to advertising to hundreds of television channels—and then they are getting penalized for getting distracted.

- In the same way that we were affected by the world we grew up in, so too have the digital generations been affected by the world they are growing up in. That world is very different from the world that we experienced as children. Like us, the digital generations have a cultural brain—a brain that reflects the culture they are living in and the experiences they are having.

- To be effective 21st century teachers, we must first possess the new basic skills our students are increasingly expected to have as the minimum requirement for survival in the culture of the 21st century. Learning is far more about *headware* than it is about *hardware*.

- The purpose of education is not to *make* students learn; it's about getting students to *want* to learn. Without motivation, there will be no learning.

- What we desperately need is *balance* between our world and theirs—between traditional and digital learning environments.

Questions to Consider

Now that you've finished the chapter, consider the following questions.

1. What are three things you know now that you did not know before you read this book?

2. What are two questions you still need to have answered?

3. What is one action you can take starting right now to move yourself, your family, your classroom, your school, and your community from where they are to where they need to be?

4. How have we modified our assumptions about teaching, learning, and assessment to address the fact that kids have fundamentally changed and continue to change?

5. What are the three reasons why organizations and individuals fail?

References and Resources

Anderson, J., & Rainie, L. (2012). *The future of gamification*. Accessed at www .pewinternet.org/Reports/2012/Future-of-Gamification/Overview.aspx on November 14, 2014.

Antranik. (2011, December 1). The eye and vision [Web log post]. Accessed at http://antranik.org/the-eye-and-vision on November 14, 2014.

Baker, F. W. (n.d.). *Media use statistics*. Accessed at www.frankwbaker.com /mediause.htm on November 14, 2014.

Beyer, B. K. (1991). *Teaching thinking skills: A handbook for elementary school teachers*. Boston: Allyn & Bacon.

Bill and Melinda Gates Foundation. (2005). *Bill Gates: National Education Summit on High Schools*. Accessed at www.gatesfoundation.org/media-center/speeches /2005/02/bill-gates-2005-national-education-summit on November 14, 2014.

Black, S. (2001). Ask me a question: How teachers use inquiry in a classroom. *American School Board Journal, 188*(5), 43–45.

Blatner, A. (2009). *Role playing in education*. Accessed at www.blatner.com/adam /pdntbk/rlplayedu.htm on November 14, 2014.

boyd, d. (2014). *It's complicated: The social lives of networked teens*. New Haven, CT: Yale University Press.

Bradley, S. (2011, February 7). 3 design layouts: Gutenberg diagram, z-pattern, and f-pattern [Web log post]. Accessed at www.vanseodesign.com/web-design /3-design-layouts on November 14, 2014.

Burmark, L. (2002). *Visual literacy: Learn to see, see to learn*. Alexandria, VA: Association for Supervision and Curriculum Development.

Chung, J. (2014). *The 10 commandments of colour theory*. Accessed at www.make
useof.com/tag/10-commandments-colour-theory on November 14, 2014.

Churches, A. (n.d.). *Bloom's digital taxonomy*. Accessed at http://edorigami
.wikispaces.com/Bloom%27s+Digital+Taxonomy on November 14, 2014.

Cisco. (2012a). *Cisco connected world technology report*. Accessed at www.cisco
.com/c/en/us/solutions/enterprise/connected-world-technology-report/index
.html#~2012 on November 14, 2014.

Cisco. (2012b). *Cisco visual networking index: Forecast and methodology, 2013–
2018*. Accessed at www.cisco.com/c/en/us/solutions/collateral/service-provider
/ip-ngn-ip-next-generation-network/white_paper_c11-481360.pdf on
November 14, 2014.

Cisco Systems. (2006). *Technology in schools: What the research says*. Accessed at
www.cisco.com/web/strategy/docs/education/TechnologyinSchoolsReport.pdf
on November 14, 2014.

Cohen, M. (2014, May 7). The invisible iPad: It's not about the device [Web log
post]. Accessed at http://blogs.kqed.org/mindshift/2014/05/the-invisible-ipad
-its-not-about-the-device on November 13, 2014.

Customer Magnetism. (n.d.). *What is an infographic?* [Infographic]. Accessed
at www.customermagnetism.com/infographics/what-is-an-infographic on
November 13, 2014.

Dredge, S. (2012, October 10). Angry Birds games have 200m monthly active
players. *The Guardian*. Accessed at www.theguardian.com/technology
/appsblog/2012/oct/10/angry-birds-200m-monthly-users on November 13,
2014.

Drucker, P. F. (2008). *The essential Drucker: The best of sixty years of Peter Drucker's
essential writings on management* (1st Collins Business Essentials paperback
ed.). New York: HarperCollins.

Eddy, M. (n.d.). *Movement in the classroom: Rationales, guidelines, and resources to
get schools moving*. Accessed at www.wellnesscke.net/downloadables
/Rationales,Strategies&ResourcesforMovementintheClassroom.pdf on
November 14, 2014.

Estes, A. C. (2014, March 11). What is the resolution of the human eye? *Gizmodo*.
Accessed at http://gizmodo.com/what-is-the-resolution-of-the-human-eye
-1541242269 on November 14, 2014.

Fast Company Staff. (2014). *The business of Facebook*. Accessed at www.fastcompany .com/1740204/business-facebook on March 15, 2015.

Fisher, D., & Frey, N. (2010). *Guided instruction: How to develop confident and successful learners*. Alexandria, VA: Association for Supervision and Curriculum Development.

Friedman, T. L. (2005). *The world is flat: A brief history of the twenty-first century*. New York: Farrar, Straus and Giroux.

Frymier, A., & Schulman, G. (1995). What's in it for me?: Increasing content relevance to enhance student motivation. *Communication Education, 44,* 40–50.

Giles, J. (2005, December 14). Internet encyclopedias go head to head. *Nature*. Accessed at www.nature.com/nature/journal/v438/n7070/full/438900a.html on March 20, 2015.

GLT Global ED. (n.d.). *About Google Lit Trips*. Accessed at www.googlelittrips .com/GoogleLit/Getting_Started.html on November 14, 2014.

Goodman, L., & Bernston, G. (2000). The art of asking good questions: Using direct inquiry in the classroom. *The American Biology Teacher, 62,* 473–476.

Graham, D. (2013, May 15). *The social revolution: Remember me* [Video file]. Accessed at www.mostwatchedtoday.com/the-social-revolution-remember-me on November 14, 2014.

Hansen, R. (2011). *Leadership and the art of surfing*. Maitlan, FL: Xulon Press.

Harris, S. (2013). 8 surprising new Instagram statistics to get the most of the picture social network [Web log post]. Accessed at https://blog.bufferapp.com /instagram-stats-instagram-tips on March 20, 2015.

Hayden, S. (2014, April 9). Why you should try video feedback with students. *Edudemic*. Accessed at www.edudemic.com/video-feedback-with-students on November 14, 2014.

Hayes, G. (n.d.). Gary's social media count [Web log post]. Accessed at www .personalizemedia.com/garys-social-media-count on November 14, 2014.

Hotz, R. (2012). When gaming is good for you. *Wall Street Journal*. Accessed at: www.wsj.com/news/articles/SB100014240529702034586045772632739431 83932 on March 20, 2014.

Hyman, L., & Schuh, R. (1974). Universals of tone rules: Evidence from West Africa. *Linguistic Inquiry, 5,* 81–115.

Immersivetech. (2010, November 11). *Crypton Future Media: Hatsune Miku—World is mine* [Video file]. Accessed at www.youtube.com/watch?v=pEaBqiLeCu0 on November 14, 2014.

Indiana University School of Education. (2010). *Schools are responding to latest findings from the High School Survey of Student Engagement.* Accessed at http://ceep.indiana.edu/hssse/pdfs/School%20of%20Education%20_%20Featu...pdf on November 14, 2014.

Jaslow, R. (2014, April 4). Cereal box characters are staring at your children, study says. *CBS News.* Accessed at www.cbsnews.com/news/cereal-box-characters-are-staring-at-your-children-study-says on November 14, 2014.

Jayanth, M. (2014). 52% of gamers are women—but the industry doesn't know it. *The Guardian.* Accessed at www.theguardian.com/commentisfree/2014/sep/18/52-percent-people-playing-games-women-industry-doesnt-know on March 20, 2015.

Johnson, B. (2013, June 28). Great teachers don't teach [Web log post]. Accessed at www.edutopia.org/blog/great-teachers-do-not-teach-ben-johnson on November 14, 2014.

Jones, S. (2014, March 10). Visual storytelling: Why data visualization is a content marketing fairytale. *Search Engine Journal.* Accessed at www.searchenginejournal.com/visual-storytelling-data-visualization-content-marketing-fairytale/92513 on November 14, 2014.

Jukes, I., McCain, T., & Crockett, L. (2010). *Understanding the digital generation: Teaching and learning in the new digital landscape.* Kelowna, British Columbia, Canada: 21st Century Fluency Project.

Juliani, A. J. (2013, June 25). Why "20% Time" is good for schools [Web log post]. *Edutopia.* Accessed at www.edutopia.org/blog/20-percent-time-a-j-juliani on November 14, 2014.

Khan Academy. (n.d.). *Coach and classroom resources.* Accessed at www.khanacademy.org/coach-res on November 14, 2014.

Knoblauch, M. (2014, April 23). Internet users send 204 million emails per minute. *Mashable.* Accessed at http://mashable.com/2014/04/23/data-online-every-minute/? on November 14, 2014.

Kumar, G. (2005). *Career excellence.* New Delhi, India: Atlantic Publishers and Distributors.

Lepi, K. (2014, March 2). What to know about using colors in the classroom. *Edudemic*. Accessed at www.edudemic.com/colors-in-the-classroom on November 14, 2014.

Lesiuk, T. (2005). The effect of music listening on work performance. *Psychology of Music, 33*(2), 173–191.

Levy, F., & Murnane, R. J. (2004). *The new division of labor: How computers are creating the next job market.* New York: Russell Sage.

Lo, B. (2010). *GPS and geocaching in education.* Eugene, OR: International Society for Technology in Education.

Louv, R. (2008). *Last child in the woods: Saving our children from nature-deficit disorder* (Updated and expanded ed.). Chapel Hill, NC: Algonquin Books.

Madrigal, A. (2012). Sorry, young man, you're not the most important demographic in tech. *Atlantic*. Accessed at www.theatlantic.com/technology /archive/2012/06/sorry-young-man-youre-not-the-most-important-demo graphic-in-tech/258087 on March 20, 2015.

Martin, A. J., & Dowson, M. (2009). Interpersonal relationships, motivation, engagement, and achievement: Yields for theory, current issues, and educational practice. *Review of Educational Research, 79*(1), 327–365.

McCain, T. (2015). *Teaching with the future in mind.* Manuscript submitted for publication.

McGonigal, J. (2011a, January 20). Playing video games can change the world. *Marketplace*. Accessed at www.marketplace.org/topics/life/big-book/playing -video-games-can-change-world on November 13, 2014.

McGonigal, J. (2011b, July 28). Video games: An hour a day is key to success in life [Web log post]. Accessed at www.huffingtonpost.com/jane-mcgonigal /video-games_b_823208.html on November 13, 2014.

Medina, J. (2008). *Brain rules: 12 principles for surviving and thriving at work, home, and school.* Seattle, WA: Pear Press.

Meister, J. (2012, August 14). Job hopping is the "new normal" for millennials: Three ways to prevent a human resource nightmare. *Forbes*. Accessed at www .forbes.com/sites/jeannemeister/2012/08/14/job-hopping-is-the-new-normal- for-millennials-three-ways-to-prevent-a-human-resource-nightmare on November 13, 2014.

Miller, C. (2013). Are schools driving ADHD diagnoses? *Child Mind Institute.* Accessed at www.childmind.org/en/posts/articles/2013-7-2-are-schools -driving-rise-adhd-diagnoses on March 20, 2015.

Murphy, M. (2013). Survey finds we're hooked on Facebook mobile. *Siliconbeat.* Accessed at www.siliconbeat.com/2013/03/29/survey-finds-were-hooked-on -facebook-mobile/ on March 20, 2015.

National Association of State Boards of Education. (2012). *Born in another time: Ensuring educational technology meets the needs of students today—and tomorrow.* Accessed at www.nasbe.org/wp-content/uploads/Born-in-Another-Time-NASB -full-report.pdf on November 13, 2014.

National Centre for Teaching and Learning of Massey University. (n.d.). *Scenario-based learning.* Accessed at www.massey.ac.nz/massey/fms/NCTL/LMS%20News /NCTL%20Website/Scenario-based-learning.pdf?107931B283F439CFB77 114AF3B9DCE03 on November 14, 2014.

National Governors Association Center for Best Practices & Council of Chief State School Officers. (2010). *Common Core State Standards for mathematics.* Accessed at www.corestandards.org on March 20, 2015.

Nickelodeon. (2013). Nickelodeon introduces "The Story of Me" research study, providing inside look at today's emerging generation of kids [Press release]. Accessed at www.prnewswire.com/news-releases/nickelodeon-introduces-the -story-of-me-research-study-providing-inside-look-at-todays-emerging -generation-of-kids-232684201.html on March 20, 2015.

The Nielsen Company. (2010). *U.S. teen mobile report calling yesterday, texting today, using apps tomorrow.* Accessed at www.nielsen.com/us/en/insights /news/2010/u-s-teen-mobile-report-calling-yesterday-texting-today-using -apps-tomorrow.html on June 3, 2015.

Nielsen, J. (2006). *F-shaped pattern for reading web content.* Accessed at www .nngroup.com/articles/f-shaped-pattern-reading-web-content on November 13, 2014.

North Central Regional Educational Laboratory, & Metiri Group. (2003). *enGauge 21st Century Skills: Literacy in the digital age.* Naperville, IL: North Central Regional Educational Laboratory.

Novak, G. (2014, March 6). Just-in-time teaching: An interactive engagement pedagogy [Web log post]. Accessed at www.edutopia.org/blog/just-in-time -teaching-gregor-novak on November 14, 2014.

OnlineCollege.org. (2012). *99 ways you should be using Facebook in your classroom [Updated].* Accessed at www.onlinecollege.org/2012/05/21/100-ways-you -should-be-using-facebook-in-your-classroom-updated on November 14, 2014.

Padnani, A. (2012, August 11). The power of music, tapped in a cubicle. *The New York Times.* Accessed at www.nytimes.com/2012/08/12/jobs/how-music-can -improve-worker-productivity-workstation.html?_r=1& on November 13, 2014.

Postman, N., & Weingartner, C. (1969). Teaching as a subversive activity. *NASSP Bulletin 53; 40,* 120–122.

Powers, J. (2010). Devising a course to bridge classroom to real world. *New York Teacher, LI*(13). Accessed at www.uft.org/teacher-teacher/devising-course -bridge-classroom-real-world on November 14, 2014.

Phys.org. (2014). *TED online archive reveals new-look website.* Accessed at http:// phys.org/news/2014-03-ted-online-archive-reveals-new-look.html on March 20, 2015.

Ratey, J. J. (2008). *Spark: The revolutionary new science of exercise and the brain.* New York: Little, Brown.

Ripp, P. (2011, October 25). So you want to do Mystery Skype? [Web log post]. Accessed at http://pernillesripp.com/2011/10/25/so-you-want-to-do-mystery -skype on November 14, 2014.

Robinson, K. (2013). How to escape education's death valley [Video file]. *TED.* Accessed at www.ted.com/talks/ken_robinson_how_to_escape_education_s _death_valley/transcript?language=en on March 20, 2015.

Rosen, L. D. (2010). *Rewired: Understanding the iGeneration and the way they learn.* New York: Palgrave Macmillan.

Ryssdal, K. (2011). Playing video games can change the world. *Marketplace.* Accessed at www.marketplace.org/topics/life/big-book/playing-video-games -can-change-world on March 20, 2015.

Schaaf, R., & Mohan, N. (2014). *Making school a game worth playing: Digital games in the classroom.* Thousand Oaks, CA: Corwin Press.

Simons, D. (2010, May 10). The monkey business illusion [Web log post]. Accessed at http://theinvisiblegorilla.com/blog/2010/05/10/the-monkey -business-illusion on November 14, 2014.

Small, G., & Vorgan, G. (2008). *iBrain: Surviving the technological alteration of the modern mind.* New York: Collins Living.

Smith, C. (2014a). *By the numbers: 26 amazing Snapchat statistics.* Accessed at http://expandedramblings.com/index.php/snapchat-statistics/# .U5qVShZ0FQ0 on November 14, 2014.

Smith, C. (2014b). *By the numbers: 60 amazing YouTube statistics.* Accessed at http://expandedramblings.com/index.php/youtube-statistics/# .U5qU5RZ0FQ0 on November 14, 2014.

Smith, C. (2014c). *By the numbers: 100+ interesting Instagram statistics.* Accessed at http://expandedramblings.com/index.php/important-instagram-stats/# .U2qSg61dU01 on November 14, 2014.

Smith, C. (2014d). *By the numbers: 250+ amazing Twitter statistics.* Accessed at http://expandedramblings.com/index.php/march-2013-by-the-numbers-a-few -amazing-twitter-stats/#.U8iJKla-ZQ0 on November 14, 2014.

Smith, C. (2015). By the numbers: 200+ amazing Facebook user statistics. *DMR.* Accessed from expandedramblings.com/index.php/by-the-numbers-17 -amazing-facebook-stats on March 5, 2015.

Smith, G. (2013). *24 essential mind mapping and brainstorming tools.* Accessed at http://mashable.com/2013/09/25/mind-mapping-tools on November 14, 2014.

TCI. (2010). *Visual discovery in five easy steps* [Presentation]. Accessed at www .teachtci.com/pdf/webinar_handouts/Visual_Discovery_Secondary.pdf on November 14, 2014.

Terdiman, D. (2005, December 15). Study: Wikipedia as accurate as Britannica. *CNET News.* Accessed at http://news.cnet.com/Study-Wikipedia-as-accurate -as-Britannica/2100-1038_3-5997332.html on November 13, 2014.

Thornburg, D. D. (1992). *Edutrends 2010: Restructuring, technology, and the future of education.* Creston, British Columbia, Canada: Starsong.

Verini, J. (2012). How virtual pop star Hatsune Miku blew up in Japan. *Wired.* Accessed at www.wired.com/2012/10/mf-japan-pop-star-hatsune-miku/ on March 20, 2015.

Vogel, D. R., Dickson, G. W., & Lehman, J. A. (1986). *Persuasion and the role of visual presentation support: The UM/3M study* (Working Paper No. MISRC-WP-86-11). Minneapolis, MN: Management Information Systems Research Center. Accessed at http://misrc.umn.edu/workingpapers /fullpapers/1986/8611.pdf on November 13, 2014.

Wikipedia: Statistics. (n.d.). In *Wikipedia*. Accessed at http://en.wikipedia.org/wiki/Wikipedia:Statistics#Edits on November 14, 2014.

Wilen, W. W. (1985). Questioning, thinking and effective citizenship. *Social Science Record, 22*(1), 4–6.

Wurman, R. S. (1989). *Information anxiety*. New York: Doubleday.

YouTube. (n.d.). *Statistics*. Accessed at www.youtube.com/yt/press/statistics.html on November 13, 2014.

Index

Deeper Learning
Edited by James A. Bellanca
Education authorities from around the globe draw on research as well as their own experience to explore deeper learning, a process that promotes higher-order thinking, reasoning, and problem solving to better educate students and prepare them for college and careers.
BKF622

Bringing Innovation to School
Suzie Boss
Activate your students' creativity and problem-solving potential with breakthrough learning projects. Across all grades and content areas, student-driven, collaborative projects will teach students how to generate innovative ideas and then put them into action.
BKF546

Contemporary Perspectives on Literacy series
Edited by Heidi Hayes Jacobs
Today's students must be prepared to compete in a global society in which cultures, economies, and people are constantly connected. The authors explain three "new literacies"—digital, media, and global—and provide practical tips for incorporating these literacies into the traditional curriculum.
BKF441, BKF235, BKF236, BKF415

Solutions for Digital Learner–Centered Classrooms series
Gain practical, high-impact strategies to enhance instruction and heighten student achievement in 21st century classrooms. Using tech-based tools and techniques, your staff will discover how to motivate students to develop curiosity, become actively engaged, and have a sense of purpose in their education.
BKF691, BKF680, BKF636, BKF679, BKF681, BKF664, BKF666

Solution Tree | Press
a division of

Solution Tree

Visit solution-tree.com or call 800.733.6786 to order.

" WOW!

I liked how I was given an effective, organized plan to help EVERY child. "